ALLERGIC
TO
AVERAGE

FROM AUTHOR
CASSIE HOWARD

Book design by *Inkstain Design Studio*

Cover design by *Regina Wamba of ReginaWamba.com*

TABLE OF CONTENTS

ALLERGIC
TO
AVERAGE

INTRODUCTION

This is a book for all of the rule-breakers, the black sheep, the driven and ambitious AF entrepreneurs. I know that you have big dreams but are scared to death that they'll never happen. You want to change the world with your words, and live life on your terms. You're ready, now, to truly be, do and have EVERYTHING you want. You have the skills and the determination, but you're struggling to figure out how to put it all together and build a mother-fucking empire.

Your family doesn't "get it". Neither does your partner. Neither do some of your closest friends. But you KNOW that you were born to do something big in this world. You are astutely aware that you're on this earth to do incredible things. The dreams are there, but you can't seem to figure out how to make them come to life. You've been trying for years and keep ending up in the same spot: clueless and overwhelmed.

You're feeling unsure of yourself, and completely exhausted. You're working day & night, trying to get your business and life to where you want it to be, refusing sleep, refusing time with family and friends, refusing.. just about everything, really, and you still feel so far away from achieving your goals.

And it's true, you get your hustle on. You do the work. You're writing and speaking and creating and selling and sharing. You're doing all the THINGS, but you're not consistent, it's starting to become boring, and it doesn't feel fun anymore.

The problem is, if you continue to do what you're doing, you'll continue to stay where you're at. Staying the same will hold you back from getting to the place that you really want to go and it will prevent you from achieving all you that you desire in your lifetime. If you don't learn to overcome your challenges and to discover exactly what needs to be done to accomplish what you set out to do, you're never going to be able to live the life you most want to live - and that would just be a tragedy, don't you think?

The truth is, you've been playing small. Thinking small. Maybe there are people in your life that are encouraging you to STAY small, so that they don't feel inadequate or for whatever other insecure reasoning they may have. There is never a time for you to play small.. you're here to play big! Do big things, see big things, achieve big things, receive big things! This is your time, right now. No more waiting.

I feel you. I remember what it was like to have the dream of getting paid to "do nothing" (meaning: getting paid just to be myself), thinking it was impossible and that it would never happen, while deep down, believing it just might - and now, that is my reality. However, it took me over a decade to get here. A decade of sacrifice and struggle that I didn't have to endure. Loss of time with my kids, failed relationships, excessive weight gain, extreme depression, debilitating debt… all because I didn't know it could be easy.

Once I learned that success could be easy, that I could make money all day, every day, just to do what I love the most, everything changed. The way I presented myself to the world changed, the way I spoke to myself changed, the way I showed up for my audience changed, and most importantly, my mindset changed. That's when life became a whole lot sweeter.

Were you ever taught that success was "hard"? That you had to work non-stop in order to become rich? That you had to sacrifice things you love in order to have the dream life you desire? In this book, I'm not only going to prove to you that those things are all total bullshit, but I'm also going to share with you the lessons I've learned about success, money, and living a fulfilled life, that you can apply to your own life, right now.

The life of your dreams is right around the corner. Are you ready for it?

I recommend that you make notes as you go through this book. Get out your journal and write down any ah-ha's you have, or anything else you want to remember.

CHAPTER 1

GETTING PAID TO BE ME

t all started innocently enough.

Here I was, a 17-year old girl, blogging on the internet, with no clue of what was about to happen in her life. Things were about to get seriously awesome, seriously fast.

I'd graduated from writing about what boys I liked in my paper diaries to sharing my life events, my thoughts, and my dreams, on the internet - no paper and pen necessary. I wasn't doing it to make money, I was doing it because I enjoyed it.

To be honest, I just loved the attention. I loved knowing that other people were reading what I was writing, even if it was only a few hundred people (at most) back at that point.

I've always been an introvert, so it was kind of fun and kind of naughty for me to share so openly online, which is probably why I liked it so much. I've always had that naughty streak and that's one of the main reasons I believe that I've been so successful in business over the years. I do what others say I can't or that I shouldn't, and it makes me money.

I've always been the rule-breaker, doing what I want! I have no space in my life for people who try to stop me from doing what lights me up.

I was blogging for awhile when I was approached by a man through email, asking me if he could pay me to share some naughty photos of myself. I was flattered and kind of turned on at the fact that someone who didn't know me wanted to see me naked... and of course, naughty is definitely something I was a fan of, so I said yes with zero hesitation.

Since my blog wasn't a business at the time, and I didn't have any way for him to send me actual money, I created a Wish List of items I wanted on Amazon. He bought me something off of my Amazon Wish List for some grainy webcam photos and it got the wheels turning in my head. I wondered if other people wanted these kinds of photos, too. I'd already taken them, so all I really had to do was mention that they were for sale and I could get even more free stuff!

I did this again and again for the same person, plus more people who came to me later, asking for photos.

That's when it all started to get real.

I took photos for more and more people, and received even more gifts from people all over the world. It was fun and exciting, but I was ready for money, not just CD's and DVD's from Amazon.

I saw other girls creating their own websites dedicated to sharing photos and videos of themselves with their "fans". I was still 17 at the time, so I wasn't able to get my own credit card to register for a domain name and pay for hosting on a website, so one of the guys who was a regular buyer of my photos actually gave me his credit card information and told me to buy whatever I wanted.

He didn't even question that I may take all of his money and run. He thought of me as his girlfriend. He trusted me. He wanted to serve me. It was in this moment that I realized I had ALL the power. I was in control of my life now. I had people bending over backwards for ME. It was exhilarating!

I paid for the domain name. I paid for hosting.

And then I got to work.

I created lots of photos, lots of videos, and started interacting with potential clients/fans on adult forums, promoting my website whenever and wherever possible. It was really easy to sell myself and I got sign-ups consistently. Eventually I had hundreds of members in my "solo-girl" website that paid me a monthly fee to receive weekly photos, videos and a live cam show.

All I needed to do was be myself and show up for my audience, and the money would flow. I couldn't believe how easy it was and was honestly quite shocked that more people didn't do this.

Lesson #1 I learned from the adult industry:

All I had to do to make money was be me.

I just had to be myself. Being ME was enough.

I didn't have to wear costumes or pretend to be someone I wasn't. I just needed to be me, and I needed to show up, and people would pay me.

It was the easiest money I ever made...

Until it wasn't.

Quickly, I made friends with a few key players in the adult industry. Some of them would even fly me out to where they were located AND pay me to do shoots for them and their communities. It was so much fun and I got paid thousands of dollars just to pose for photos for a day or two.

Contrary to popular belief, people in the adult industry are some of the nicest, most genuine people you will ever meet. The men aren't dirty pigs and the women aren't arrogant bitches. Everyone I ever met was so kind and extremely respectful.

It was really easy to make friends and no one ever made you feel like you weren't good enough to hang out with them (even if you were a "newbie" to the industry). I spent time with industry leaders who were making tens of millions of dollars each year and also with people who were grateful to make a few grand each month and they all treated me the same.

Doing this work was fun, but I was starting to get really tired.

I was taking photos every day. I had to constantly get my hair and nails done. I had to buy new outfits all of the time. It was exhausting, and cost me a ton of money to keep it all up. As much as I enjoyed being the star, I realized that I didn't want to be the star if that meant I was required to constantly be "on".

Eventually, I started to get behind the camera and spent less time in front of it.

There is SO much money to be made in the adult industry, and I knew that one way to make a lot of it, without actually being a model

4

myself, was to be the photographer. So that's what I did! I decided to shoot other models, and sell the photos to friends of mine who had large adult membership sites.

Lesson #2 I learned from the adult industry:
Make friends with people who are further along than
you are. Learn from them. Let them help you.

Although it was easy work, it wasn't all easy. I had to deal with models who didn't show up, or who did show up, but who looked way different than the photos they'd posted online. I had to deal with content that no one wanted to buy because my lighting wasn't good enough or I didn't have enough ass close-ups. The money, however, was so good and worth the occasional pain-in-the-ass client or model.

I was taking thousands of dollars doing this work. I was living on my own, paying all of my bills, totally independent. It was normal for me to spend hundreds of dollars on tanning, nails, make-up, hair styling, and clothing for my own modelling, and thousands of dollars paying my models. I travelled to adult events where I could get my name out there because I knew that would make me more money. My life was so fun and exciting!

Working in the adult industry is one of the best things I've ever done. It was fun, it was exciting, it was easy (most of the time), and all I had to do to make money was be me. I learned so much about myself and also about business while being an adult model and photographer. I can definitely say, hands down, it was the most fun I've ever had at a "job" before!

I knew that a lot of people in my life wouldn't understand

or accept the fact that I made my money by getting naked on the internet. Sex was seen as something dirty. Selling yourself made you a whore, even if you weren't having sex with strangers and were just taking pictures of yourself, naked in your bedroom.

So of course, when my parents found out that this is how I was making so much money, shit hit the fan!

My mom even had the internet shut off at our house to stop me from posting on there. I just used the internet at the library and at friends houses, saved up my money, and moved into my own apartment.

I wasn't going to let anything or anyone stop me from doing what I wanted to do.

I had other family members talk about me behind my back (and some right to my face) about how I was "disgusting" and that what I was doing was so wrong and shameful. Sex is supposed to be private! Your naked body is only reserved for your husband!

Um... no. My naked body is mine to do with what I please. And I loved showing it off, so that's exactly what I did. Eventually, they gave up trying to convince me to quit and just started acting as though it wasn't happening.

Lesson #3 I learned from the adult industry:
Do what you enjoy, even if other people don't understand it.
Fuck the naysayers.

And then... I did my taxes for the year. I owed around $10,000 because I hadn't been making payments all year long. And then, soon after this discovery, I received my credit card statement in the mail. My card was maxed out. Another $10,000 owing. That's $20,000 I was in the hole and was expected to pay right then and there.

It was like a punch to the gut.

I didn't have $20,000 to spare. I didn't even have $5,000. I barely had enough money to pay for my basic living expenses at that point!

After years of modelling and shooting, receiving thousands and thousands of dollars each year, I never once thought to manage my money. Why wasn't I taught basic money-management skills in school? How was I so clueless?

I was so excited to see it coming in, and in larger amounts than I'd ever seen hit my account before, that I spent it as soon as I received it.

It all added up and now I was $20,000 in debt and freaking out about whether or not I'd be able to make rent that month.

Talk about a scary experience.

I reached out to one of my friends in the adult industry about it, and he offered to pay me $20,000 to buy my solo site. That meant he would have all of my personal photos, videos, community, recorded shows.. and I would no longer own it.

In short: I had to sell me again, but this time, I wouldn't ever be able to get "me" back. Once I said yes to this offer, that content no longer belonged to me. It was such a painful thought... what if I wanted to take that content down one day - especially if I had kids - and I couldn't do it?

I thought about it for a long while, but ultimately, I said yes to the $20,000 deal. I needed the money.

And just like that, all of my content was gone. I couldn't make money from it any longer. I was back to square one.

Lesson #4 I learned from the adult industry:
Manage your money. Pay attention to it. Set aside cash for taxes. Pay off your credit cards. Live within your means.

What I now know to be true is this: Everything I know about business, I learned from the adult industry.

Working in the adult industry, seeing how actors and actresses made their money, spending time with those who have been in this line of work for many years, taught me so much about what is possible in regards to creating a business and a lifestyle that I love. I didn't have to struggle or do things I didn't want to do. I could just be me, and that was enough.

It was one of the most transformative and eye-opening experiences of my life, and I know, is what ultimately led me to doing what I do now, inspiring others to make money being themselves, in the way that brings them the most joy. If I could go back and do it all over again, I would do so in a heartbeat, without thinking twice.

I look back on this period of my life and the word that comes to mind for me is GRATEFUL. I am so damn grateful for this industry and all that it taught me.

Thank you, adult industry, for the fun you showed me I could have.

Thank you, adult industry, for the lessons you taught me about business (and life).

Thank you, adult industry, for the strength you gave me in owning who I am.

Thank you, adult industry, for giving me all I needed to live life on my terms, unapologetically. You made me a stronger, more confident person, and I'll always love you and sing your praises for this.

I know I've said this a bunch of times already, but it's incredibly important, so I'm going to say it again:

Working in the adult industry was so much fun! I was having fun all of the time, and the more fun I had, the more money I made. It was like FUN was the secret ingredient to success and it was working out in my favor in a massive way.

I had fun taking photos, doing my weekly shows, hanging out with other adult models, going to events... it was honestly the most exciting few years ever! I never thought that making money could be so enjoyable, but gratefully, it was.

> Lesson #5 I learned from the adult industry:
> Money follows fun. The more fun you have,
> the more money you make.

I'll never forget this period of my life; the time when everything changed for me. It was during this time when I learned what was possible and what I was capable of. Even though many people don't understand it, I truly believe and know that the adult industry changed my life for the better.

I wouldn't be where I am today had I not said YES to sending off those initial photos and then creating a whole tribe of raving fans and followers that would pay me to do just about anything I felt like doing.

Working in the adult industry was exciting, I enjoyed every minute of it, and am forever grateful for it, but it also led me down a very dark path....

CHAPTER 2

MONEY, AND THE HAVING OF IT

The thing about money, is that it's really not as complicated as everyone makes it out to be. Money, and the having of it, is honestly quite simple.

DO THINGS THAT MAKE YOU MONEY. I mean, really, anything, so long as it sets your soul on fire. There are so many ways that you can make money today. The internet has made the possibilities endless. People who never finished high school are creating 6 and 7-figure businesses. People who have never once created any kind of physical product are building clothing empires.

There are people all over the world, doing things they love, and making incredible money doing so. It's like all of a sudden there was this big 'ol magic SUCCESS button, and every day, someone hit it and achieved the success they desired. People with far less experience than you, far less ambition than you, far less money than you, far less drive than you.

You have talents and skills and value worth sharing, and they are worthy of incredible amounts of money. Everyone is born with a gift inside of them to share. Are you willing to share your gifts with the world?

Are you willing to get paid to be YOU, to do great work, to change lives? Good news: You can do that, and you can do that today. Just start.

ACTION ITEM: *Brainstorm a list of 30 different ways that you can make money in the next 60 days. Get creative. Think outside of the box.*

KEEP TRACK OF, AND PAY, YOUR BILLS. I mean, I hate to even bring this up because it just seems so obvious, but I can't tell you how many times people tell me they can't pay their bills, and so, they don't. I am guilty of this myself, as well. I avoided my debts and my bills like the plague. I wouldn't touch them and simply pretended that they didn't exist.

This is a very bad idea.

Take care of your bills. Respect those who performed a service for you, or who sold a product to you, by honouring your commitment and paying your bills. If you really, truly, don't have the money to take care of your bills in full, you may need to start a payment plan. You may need to make small payments to start.. and that's okay.

Be grateful for what you spent that money on, it was worth it to you at the time you made the decision to purchase it.

Debt is neither good nor bad. It's just… debt. It's a decision you made to put an item or service or item on a credit card in the past. Same goes for mortgages, lines of credit, loans from the bank, friends, family… these were CHOICES you made, that's all. Nothing to beat yourself up about.

One of the best things that ever happened to me (over and over) is debt. Losing money, owing people, and being fearful of ever receiving money again. I'm so GRATEFUL that I had this experience when I was young, so I could learn from it, and do differently in my adult years.

Over $30K in debt, I knew something had to change. It was a wake-up call for me, and I'm so glad it happened because it gave me the kick in the ass I needed to get my money situation sorted. It's still a work in progress, as I believe it ALWAYS will, but I'm definitely way better than I was 10+ years ago when I was in the face with that huge debt amount!

Debt isn't the devil, it's not something to run and hide from. In fact, I LOVE debt and the opportunities it provides me.

Debt allowed me to start my first business.

Debt allowed me to hire my first business coach and learn a TON about marketing and mindset.

Debt allowed me to hire my second, third and fourth business coach and learn even MORE (about money, business, lifestyle and more).

Of course, I now PAY off my debt whenever I accumulate it, but I don't ever let myself use the words "I can't afford it" when something I desire is presented in front of me. If it will help me make more money, I'll go into debt for it (if necessary). That's basically my only rule when it comes to debt.

Oh, and side note: If you don't pay your bills on time, don't expect your clients to pay their bills (including you) on time. What you give, you receive. What you don't give, you don't receive.

ACTION ITEM: *Set up an auto-withdrawal from your bank account to put money toward any debts every week or month. Decide on an amount for each debt, set up the auto-pay, and leave it alone. Pay more when you want to. And then, forget about it. Do NOT focus on how much debt you have as this will just reinforce debt in your life, and thus, create more of it.*

MAKE SURE YOU'RE PUTTING MONEY ASIDE IN SAVINGS. Even if all you can afford right now is $10 per week to put into a savings account, do it. This gets your mindset into a place of abundance, because it sees money available (the amount is unimportant.. if there's money available - any amount - you are abundant). At which point, you FEEL abundant, and from there, you can create even more of it in your life.

I have a business savings account where, every week, $500 is automatically taken from my checking account, and put into it. I spent 10 minutes on the phone with the bank to set this up, and then it was done. Now I can update the amount through online banking any time I want, but in the meantime, at least $500 per week goes into business savings. My goal is to eventually be saving $10,000 per month in my business, and I know that day isn't far off!

I know you may feel like you don't have "enough" money to save anything, thinking you'll wait until you're making more before you make savings a priority. Or maybe you've been told that you need to pay your debts before you save your money because the interest you'd be paying on debts wasn't worth it, and while.. yeah, you'll pay a lot more in interest on credit cards than you will in money earned from savings, know this:

When you save money, you're telling the universe that, even though you have debt, YOU are a priority, and in turn, the universe makes you a priority, and starts bringing you more of what you desire.

I definitely believe you want to put more money toward your debt than into savings - get that paid off as soon as humanly possible - but don't neglect your own sense of financial safety and security that a savings account will provide (even a small one).

Savings isn't sexy, but it's necessary.

ACTION ITEM: *Set up an automatic savings plan for your business (and possibly for your personal banking as well). YOU are important, and so is your financial well-being. Savings helps with that.*
ALWAYS PAY YOURSELF BEFORE YOU PAY ANYONE ELSE.

I'm talking before you pay any bills, before you pay your team, before you pay for THINGS. Always pay yourself first. Decide on a set monthly amount that you commit to paying yourself every single month, consistently (you can always pay yourself MORE, but never less than the committed amount).

If possible, have this amount automatically transferred into your personal bank account each month, either monthly or weekly, so you don't have the opportunity to give yourself any bullshit excuses as to why you can't afford to pay yourself this month. You can, and you will.

I personally have a set monthly payroll amount automatically transferred into my bank account every month, and then at the very end of the month, if I want to take out any more money from the business, I will write myself a check and mark it as "dividends".

Don't believe anyone who tells you that you have to go a year or two (or whatever the number is) without making any money in your business before you start making a profit and can pay yourself. That is total and utter crap. Pay yourself now. It may not be much, but that's not the point. What you're really doing by paying yourself first is PUTTING yourself first.

And yes, you come first.

Before you can help and serve and lead others, you need to first take care of you. And that includes taking care of your money.

ACTION ITEM: *Set up an automatic payment each month that goes toward paying yourself. Aim to do this within the first week of each month, or do weekly payments if that works better. Figure out how much money you need each month, tack on a little extra, and set it up so that you get paid that amount monthly, on repeat. No more being paid last (which, if we're being honest here, usually means not getting paid at all, am I right?!).*

FOCUS ON INVESTING YOUR MONEY SO THAT IT CAN GROW.
I know it's tempting to want to spend all of that money as it comes in, but the worst thing you can do is get rid of it. Even saving money isn't enough. You need to INVEST you r money, too, and wisely.

Invest in the things that interest you, that you understand, and that you know you will get a return on.

Some great things to invest in:

- Private mentorship with someone to help you grow your business/money
- Real estate
- Stocks / bonds
- Other businesses

Like I said, make sure you UNDERSTAND these things, otherwise, you may as well just flush your hard-earned cash down the toilet and say goodbye. Do your research. Learn what you need to learn in order to capitalize on these great money-making opportunities. Not everyone who invests is gonna get a return on their investments. Don't let yourself fall into that category.

The more you know, the more you earn.

ACTION ITEM: *Come up with 3 different ways you can invest your money right now. Choose the 1 that stands out most to you (right now), and commit 1 hour per day learning about it. Don't forget to take action on what you learn!*

The one thing anyone with money can tell you is that if you want to have it, you have to give it the attention that it deserves. You have to make time for it, make space for it, be open to the receiving of it. Only then can you expect to not only have it, but keep it, and multiply it.

What you think and feel and believe about money is exactly what is mirrored back to you.

If you believe money is hard to make, money will be hard to make. If you believe it's unlimited, and you can have and circulate as much of it as you want, then that's what you will experience.

You can make what you want, save what you want, give what you want, with no limits, if you believe that to be true.

So let me ask you: What do you believe to be true about money? Go ahead and write down everything that comes to you. Here's what most people will write when they do this exercise:

- Making money takes forever.
- I could never be rich.
- My family never had money, so I will never have money.
- I don't know how to make more money.
- I can't save money.
- It's too hard to make the money I want to make.
- Making a lot of money means I need to sacrifice time with my family & friends.
- Only selfish people want to be rich.
- I need to save money in case it runs out.
- Sure, SHE can be rich, but not me. I'm not ____ enough.

And so on and so forth. How many of these beliefs/thoughts do you resonate with. It's okay, don't be shy or try to deny your feelings. The first step to getting better is first admitting what is wrong. Right now? That's your thoughts around money, abundance, and success.

It's time to change that.

A new question to ask yourself is "how do I WANT to feel about money?".. what comes up for you when you ask yourself that question?

Maybe you think:

- I love money and it loves me back!
- It's so damn easy to make $___ every month!
- I am wealthy!
- I am worthy of unlimited abundance!
- Money flows into my life every day, with total ease!

- I always have money available to me whenever I need or want it!
- It's so easy for me to save and hold on to money!
- My income grows quickly, month after month!
- The more money I make, the more good I can do in the world!
- I make money at the snap of my fingers!
- I always know exactly what to say & do to make money when I want to!

And on and on.

See how this works? Change your thoughts. Change your beliefs. And in doing so, you will change your reality.

The person who loves money, who respects it, who appreciates it, who pays attention to it, is the person who receives it (and holds on to what they want of it - not out of fear or scarcity, but to give themselves the gift of feeling more abundant).

Let me share with you a money story that I was recently telling myself, that put me out $120,000 and almost killed my marriage.

Just over a year ago, I decided I needed to live in a big house. I kept telling myself that a big house would make me happy and that I deserved it, so I should have it. Not only did I want a big house, I wanted a big house in a completely different city - one of the priciest cities in all of Canada.

Being in this city will make me feel abundant, I told myself.

Being in the big house will make me attract more money, I'd say to my husband.

I searched and searched for THE house. They were all either way too small (or in a bad area) or way too ugly. Or they were 8,000 square feet and up. I didn't want to settle. I didn't want the small house. I didn't want the ugly house. I didn't want the house in the "wrong" area.

So I went for the big house. The 8,000 square foot house that was $10,000 a month and way too big for us - because I deserved it, of course.

But really, if I'm being honest, because I wanted to show off. I wanted people to think I was special. I wanted to feel like a "rich person". I wanted to impress others.

The house was nice, don't get me wrong. I really, truly, loved the home and the neighbourhood was absolutely perfect, but after just a month of living there, I knew we wouldn't live there past the one year lease. And we didn't. Around the 6-month mark, I gave the agent a heads up that we wouldn't be renewing our lease. He tried to get us to stay, the owners of the home loved us because we didn't bother them and we paid our rent on time, but I knew that we couldn't. This wasn't the house for us and I had to let it go.

It was a depressing year in that house. One of the hardest of my life. I've never fought so much with my husband, who was furious that I'd made such a selfish decision without any consideration for his thoughts on the matter (which were: "the house is way too freakin' big for us, this is a terrible idea!"), as I did during the 12 months we lived in this house. We even talked about divorce and whether or not I was capable of managing money at all.

I felt guilty all the time.

I doubted my ability to make any good decision about anything.

My income tanked because I felt so shitty about money.

I accumulated debt on top of more debt, until I had over $50,000 owing.

I was so ashamed and felt so horrible about what I'd done.

I beat myself up for a long time, but eventually I knew that I had to forgive myself and move on if I was ever gonna dig myself out of the whole I was being buried alive in. And so I did. I clawed my way back out, stronger than ever before.

We started looking for a new home and somehow, within a short window of time, found one that is perfect for us, just a few blocks away from the castle we lived in last. We're now all settled in and I couldn't be happier. It's exactly where we're meant to be right now, and I'm proud of myself for getting up off the ground, dusting myself off, and moving forward, after such a shitty experience around money and what I really, truly want - which is NOT a giant home, I've discovered,

What you need to know about money is this:

It's there. It's always available to you. You're free to access the endless stream of it whenever you so choose. Don't deny yourself the opportunity of unlimited abundance.

Give money attention. Forgive yourself for past mistakes you made. Take action every day toward what you want.

If a broke Crazy Coupon Lady can go from big black hole of debt and zero understanding of how to create wealth, to a half-a-million dollar yearly business (and growing), you too can have abundance in your life. Trust yourself. You can do this.

CHAPTER 3

STAY TRUE TO YOU

I couldn't stop worrying about my future. It consumed every moment of every day. When was the next unexpected bill going to show up? When was I going to get kicked out of my house because I didn't pay the rent on time? When was I going to be free of debt? WOULD I ever be free of debt? Would I ever live my dream of being financially free?

The fear of being completely broke forever and constantly living with debt freaked me the fuck out.

I didn't want that. I was terrified. Anyone I talked to about it (which wasn't very many people because the embarrassment kept me quiet) told me I needed to lower my expenses, so I took a look at the bills I was paying.

Turned out, they weren't the problem. The problem was that I simply wasn't bringing enough money to live the lifestyle I wanted to live.

I had a decision to make. I could either lower my standards of living to save money, or I could find a way to make *more* money, and continue living the lifestyle I was accustomed to and enjoyed.

I decided to go the "make more money" route.

I remember opening up Google that day and searching "how to make money online". There were a ton of ideas, many of which I had no interest in, but my creative juices were flowing. I browsed page after page, site after site, until I stumbled upon a blog that mentioned extreme couponing. In the description, the blogger detailed how she was able to receive over $1,000 in groceries for less than $100. Intrigued, I clicked the link and read the post in its entirety.

That, quite honestly, is how I got into couponing.

Even though the blog I had stumbled across was an American blog, and so all of the deals and strategies she shared were only for US residents, I knew there had to be something like this available in Canada.

Turns out, there wasn't. There were deal sites and coupon sides, but nothing that was personalized - nothing that was simply one person, sharing who she was, giving details on the shopping hauls she planned and experienced. I wanted to learn from a person not from a company (even if many of those deal sites were run by just one person, you couldn't tell, because they never talked about themselves, it was strictly business). I decided that person would be me.

And that's how Mrs January was quickly flipped from a personal blog to a frugal living and couponing website. I went from talking about boys I liked and what I ate for lunch, to how to get free stuff mailed to you, how to save over 50% off your grocery bill, and how to get stores to pay YOU to buy from them.

The thing that set my blog apart from the other sites that shared deals, coupons, and freebies, is that I was sharing my own personal story. I WAS the brand. I spoke to my readers as though I was speaking to a friend, and I was open and honest with them about everything.

I let them into my life.

Shared about my marriage (and taught them "How To Save Money On Your Wedding"), about parenting, my kids, my lifestyle.

I brought them along with me (via video, since live-streaming wasn't a thing yet) when I went shopping and showed them how I put deals together and where to find hidden sale items.

I was an open book - and it worked. My readers started to trust me, listen to me, and like me. I had created a connection with them, one that made them visit my blog over the other sites that were out there.

Building my community wasn't easy at first. Before I could grow, I needed to know how to use coupons myself, and then bring my audience along with me on my journey to mastering this skill. Plus, I didn't even plan on making money from my audience. I just wanted to get free stuff myself! If I could help others in the process, that was a bonus.

I started couponing out of necessity. I needed the free stuff that coupons would get me, so that I could spend my money on other things that there weren't coupons for (you know, like rent?). So I sat down, and I got to work.

First, I went through all of the couponing blogs that I could find for Canadians and I printed and ordered all of the coupons I could find. I made note of how they matched up sales with coupons.

I wanted to know how to do it "right" so that I had the best possible chance of it working for me. I went to a bunch of different grocery stores and looked for coupons I could add to my collection. I filed them all in cute little organized file boxes. I was ready. I was prepared!

I pictured a room in my house, fill of shelving units that were loaded with groceries, toiletries, and household items. My own little grocery store that was full of stuff I paid pennies on the dollar for. It was so exciting. I saw it in my mind, and I knew it was going to happen. I just didn't believe how quickly it would become real.

Every week I ran to the door, early in the morning, when I knew that flyers would be there, and I would happily sit and read them all, highlighting all of the products I knew I had coupons for. Then, I would open up my coupon file boxes and would see how many deals I could make work. I'd match them up and make my shopping list, and then I'd hit the stores.

I couldn't believe just how easy it was! I was getting free stuff left and right, it was like my birthday every single day. I remember one deal in particular where I'd bought 108 bottles of dish soap for less than $2 (which was all taxes). The product was on sale for around $1.49 and I had a bunch of coupons for $5 off the purchase of 3 bottles. That meant, for every 3 bottles I purchased, I had $0.51 in "overage", which was applied to the tax at the end of the transaction. It was so exciting!

I shared these deals on my blog, and was having such a fun time teaching other people how to do what I was doing. Grocery shopping quickly became my new favorite thing to do. I was at the stores almost daily, hunting for deals that may or may not have been advertised (it was always a thrill when you'd find markdown items in the clearance section that you could use your coupons toward).

Eventually, that stockpile that I'd visualized and dreamed about was real. It started with just a few shelving units in my basement. Those started to overflow and we would have multiple little stockpiles around the house in order to keep the flow coming. At another home we moved into, I had the entire basement wall to use for my stockpile. I must have had 6 big shelving units full of peanut butter, diapers, Ziploc bags, and pasta alone! And the flow continued.

I was getting so much free (and almost free) stuff every day. I could barely keep up with all of the opportunities. My stockpile grew and grew.

Once we bought our own home, I wanted a dedicated stockpile room built for me. We actually built a room in our basement for the stockpile. Built-in shelving units and even a door to keep the cats and dogs out (since we stockpiled pet food, too). It was like a dream. It was the exact stockpile I'd seen in my mind when I first started couponing. This was the first time I'd noticed that I manifested something into my life through visualization and belief, but I didn't put two and two together just then. That happened much later.

Even though I was consistently showing up and posting on the blog multiple times every day, I wasn't making money. I didn't really even know *how* to make money from my blog. I just knew how to make money from couponing (get an awesome deal, keep some products for me, donate a bunch, sell the rest). It wasn't until one day

I landed on another blogger's website where she shared how much money she was making from blogging. Most of it came from ads. So, I decided to throw some ads up on my blog and see what happened. The money trickled in, but I was excited because it was money I didn't have to actively "work" for.

Over time, the money from ads on the blog grew. Eventually I was making hundreds of dollars per day just by having a couple of ads on my blog. I was curious how I could make that amount grow, so back to my dear friend Google, I went. That's when I discovered a new money-making opportunity - affiliate marketing. I spent weeks testing it out, mostly using Amazon as my main affiliate site. I would take deals from their site, post them on my blog with my unique affiliate link, and make money every time someone purchased through that link.

I still do that today.

Over time, I was making just shy of $100 per day, and during the holidays I'd make more than double that almost every day for a good month straight. November and December were always my best months for affiliate marketing since people were happily spending money on gifts for their friends and family (and let's be honest - themselves, too).

I experimented with other affiliate platforms as well, getting unique affiliate links for stores like Walmart, The Gap, Old Navy, and more. I had an affiliate link for almost every website I was already promoting deals at - only now I was getting paid to promote those deals!

Traffic to the website was growing quickly, and the money

I earned from it also grew. The bigger the website got, the more opportunities I received, and as such, the more visibility and money I received. I was featured in the news, I would get my link shared on an influencers blog (resulting in thousands of new blog readers), and I was getting paid to test and sample new products all the time.

The more I did this work, the more I showed up for my audience, the more opportunities that came my way, the more I loved it. The more I loved it, the easier it became, and the more money I would make. It was fun! It didn't feel like work at all. It was just me, being me, sharing what I was doing in my life, with the world. Life was easy. That was, of course, until I made a huge lifestyle change.

I went vegan. I decided, after watching an educational (and depressing) documentary about where our food actually comes from, that I would no longer consume animal products of any kind. It was an instant decision, and one that I've never looked back from. Going vegan is one of the best things I've ever done and I don't miss animal products at all.

The problem, though, is that once I went vegan, I couldn't use a lot of the coupons I had in my stash because they were for animal products (milk, cheese, butter, eggs, meat, etc.) or processed foods which I'd stopped eating (once you go vegan, you tend to want to be healthier all around and start craving REAL food). I also couldn't use coupons on the majority of the household items and toiletries because the products were tested on animals and I was 100% against that.

It's not that I couldn't get deals and free stuff anymore, it's that I didn't WANT most of the deals available because they were for products I wouldn't use or consume. I knew that my audience still wanted those deals, and I knew that I wanted to keep making money, so I kept promoting the deals and freebies for about a year, hiring a team to help me so that I didn't have to do it all myself. It was such easy money that I felt stupid for even considering stopping. So I kept it up. Day after day, feeling more and more like a fraud as the days went on.

Eventually, one day, I just snapped.

I looked at my coupon binder (I'd upgraded from coupon boxes!), looked at my stack of coupons that I'd been meaning to organize but never did, and I just lost it. "Fuck this shit", I said to myself, stormed over to the binder, picked it up, and threw it in the trash.

Tired is an under-statement. I was working 12+ hour days, barely around for my family and friends, trying to squeeze every last cent I could out of this blog. I was up all night and awake crazy early, posting every deal and coupon under the sun so that I could be the "first" blog to share it and my ego could grow a bit larger. It was exhausting. I was making around $100,000 per year at this point, but I didn't even care. It wasn't worth it. I couldn't do it anymore.

I felt so guilty for promoting something I didn't believe in. Even though other people believed in it, and they were able to save money and get free or cheap food from my sharing the deals and offers with them, it didn't feel right to me. Promoting an "awesome deal" on dead animals was making me sick to my stomach. Quite simply, I was acting out of alignment, and I was just plain DONE with it. I didn't want to be that person anymore - the one who hid who she truly was, just so she could make a quick buck.

Hell to the no. I was done deceiving myself. I was done deceiving others.

I decided in that money that I was going to be true to who I was. I was going to honour who I was. I was going to be ME and fuck anyone who didn't like it.

Just like that, I quit. I walked away.

I didn't tell anyone (except my team, who I let go). I just... stopped.

After I threw out my coupons, I felt like I'd just lost 20 pounds. There was this sense of weightlessness to my body. I felt free, after feeling trapped for so long. I stopped running the blog, I let go of my team soon after, and I eased into this new way of life. The one where I actually did things that felt right and good.

Once I did that, something incredible happened and my life changed again - only this time, it was a $1 Million Dollar+ change...

CHAPTER 4

FOLLOW YOUR GUT

Even though I'd stopped posting deals and coupons on the website, I was still writing blogs on various topics (usually around saving money) because I hadn't stopped enjoying THAT part. I loved writing, I loved sharing my thoughts and my experiences with others, especially if I knew it could potentially help them in some way. So I kept on writing. I kept on posting. I kept on showing up. I just stopped showing up as Cassie, The Coupon Queen and started showing up as Cassie, The Blogging Queen instead.

People were still coming to the blog every day. Over 200,000 visitors every month was consistent for months. I wrote, I wrote, and I wrote some more, but only about things that really excite me, and nothing else. I gave myself permission to be fully me, and do whatever I felt called to do, even if it didn't really make sense on paper. It was working. People were engaging. They were asking questions. They were begging for more!

At one point, I felt guided to talk about how I made money from my blog. It was something I knew a lot about, had a passion for, and knew that other people could benefit from (many of my readers were also bloggers). I hesitated for a little while because I was worried about what other people would think if I started talking about how much money I was making from my blog. I didn't want them to think that the only reason I was blogging was for money. I was terrified that I would make people upset by writing about money, since I'd always been told that talking about money was "bad" and had all kinds of negative thoughts and beliefs about money:

- Rich people are greedy
- It's wrong to take money from other people
- You have to work hard for money, it's not supposed to be easy
- Money doesn't grow on trees (another way of saying making money isn't easy)
- Only arrogant people who are full of themselves talk about money, and they do it to rub it in your face

I didn't want to be one of those people that I was worried I would somehow automatically BE just by simply talking about money. So I didn't do it. Not for awhile anyway. Until eventually, I just did. I don't even remember WHY I did. But it happened. And that's when everything started to shift.

I wrote a simple post on making money blogging, and how I was doing it myself, and had so many people comment and reach out, asking for more. So I wrote more - and I was actually having fun with it! I loved talking about this stuff, so it was only natural that it would be fun and easy for me to do. The only thing, though, is that it wasn't really making me much money. The majority of the money I made from my blog was through advertising and the deals and coupons themselves (if someone clicked my unique links). So I started using affiliate links in my blog posts around my favorite kinds of tools for making money online.

This was good enough, but eventually my income started to take a nosedive. The majority of the people who would visit my site came there for the money-saving deals, coupons, and freebies. So when I stopped sharing those things, my income went down, as expected. I tried not to focus on it, but it was hard. I wanted to make more money - I was tired of having to post links every day and if I didn't, my income would drop even quicker.

It was kind of a nightmare.

But then one day, something amazing happened, and my life changed forever. I received an email (or a comment on one of my blog posts, I can't remember) from someone, thanking me for my posts on making money blogging, and casually suggesting I should create a program that teaches people, step-by-step, how to make money blogging. She included a link to a program that someone else had created, who was doing something similar.

I thought - what the hell? What's the worse that can happen? - and I put something together.

It was one of the easiest things I've ever done, because I knew so much about this stuff. It was something that I'd done for years, and I considered myself pretty damn good at it. So putting together a program around it, didn't take me much time at all. I just did a simple brainstorm around the biggest lessons I'd learned around how to monetize a blog, and then I decided which one I would talk about each week, for the 12 weeks of the program.

The first thing I noticed when I went through this process of building my first ever program, was just how much fun it was. I was excited again - exactly how I felt when I started my original blog in the first place. It was clear that I'd lost my passion for couponing/ deal-hunting and that my new passion was talking about business & money (I mean, that's ALWAYS been a huge passion of mine, but I always used to think it was "bad" to talk about that stuff - especially making money - so I never did).

I put together a 12-week program called Money Making Mama (since, at the time, my ideal clients/students were stay-at-home moms like me), and in it, I taught how to make more money from your blog in 12 weeks or less. I priced it around $200 and launched it into the world, with glee. I was so excited to share this with the world, and also: To make a lot of money from it.

My goal was 100 women. I don't know why I chose that number, but I did. I put up post-it notes all over my office wall, all blank, and ready for the names of the 100 women who signed up (something I'd seen another woman for the launch of one of her programs). It was a fun experiment, but if I'm being honest, I never actually believed 100 women would sign up. I thought I'd be lucky if I was able to get ONE measly sign up. My lack of confidence was mind-blowing.

100 women didn't up. 50 women didn't sign up. Not even 10 women signed up. I had 7 women sign up for the program. At first, I was disappointed, but I knew that 7 was better than 0, so I practiced gratitude, and decided to give 100% to those 7 women.

Delivering the content for this program was so exciting. I was lit up, excited to talk about all things blogging, business, and money. My 3 favorite things! I was actually happy to show up and "do the work". It no longer felt like a chore that I had to endure. I woke up happy every day, excited to talk about this stuff with those 7 badass women who were committed to taking their blogs (and their business) to the next level financially. It was exhilarating.

There were days where I had to pinch myself. Did I really just get paid over $1,000 to talk about something that I would give my left arm to talk about for FREE, with anyone who'd listen? How is this real life?

It took a little while to get used to this new life I was creating. This new way of showing up and serving others. It felt easy. It felt fun. It felt way more aligned than ever before. I was happy again. I was excited. And I was just getting started.

The 12 weeks went by quickly (it's true what they say - time really does fly when you're having fun!). Each week I got more and more sad that the program was coming to an end. I didn't want it to be over. I wanted to keep sharing this stuff forever. I loved it so much, and I knew that what I was sharing was helping these women to do more, have more, be more. They were loving it, and so was I. I didn't want to stop.

Once the 12 weeks ended, I had multiple messages from the women involved, telling me how it helped them and how much they loved it (talk about an AMAZING feeling!), and asking if I was going to do another program.

I hadn't thought that far ahead, but I knew for sure that I definitely wanted to keep talking about this stuff. I wasn't at all ready to let it all go. I was back to my old self: Having fun with my business, showing up excited to do the "work", giddy to share what I was doing with everyone. I knew I couldn't quit now. I knew that this was only the beginning.

Over the 3+ years that followed (at the time of writing this book), I've launched dozens of programs around business, money, mindset and more - to the tune of $1.5 million dollars in cash received. I've been able to create, write, share, and deliver, content that makes me happy and excited to talk about. I've made money just by being myself and talking about what I love - which is living life on your terms and doing what makes you happy (and getting paid for it).

The biggest lesson I learned from this experience of launching Money Making Mama, is to always follow your gut. I listed to my intuitive nudges that pushed me toward writing more about making money blogging and from that, came people asking me for more, and to teach them how to apply this money-making goodness to their own blogs so that they could make more money, too.

My gut told me to write about making money blogging. I did. And from there, I was able to build a multiple 6-figure business that is growing exponentially. I didn't have to force myself to write about blogging or about making money because these were things that truly interested me and made excited to think and talk about, which meant that it was incredibly easy to share.

It's funny how the stuff I used to think no one would care about (like blogging and money) is the stuff that would get me to where I am today, living my dream life, getting paid to be me and do what I love. I don't ever have to write about, or create, things that don't light me up. I don't have to put on a fake smile and pretend to be someone I'm not.

All I need to do is be me, have fun, follow the nudges, and take action every day. This is how I've built my business. This is what will take me to 7-figures and beyond. The easier it gets, the more I get to receive and experience.

What you really need to understand is this:

You MUST pay attention for the signs. The nudges. The clues that are right in front of you every day (but that you don't notice). Look for them. These are your next steps, laid out for you, guiding you down the path that will take you exactly where you want to go. If you continue living your life in a way that doesn't feel good, and you're not paying attention to the guidance you're being given (and acting on it), you will continue to stay where you are. You won't get to that next level. You will continue to stay where you are - but worse still, you will TRY (and fail) at improving your life, because you're trying to force it to happen a certain way.

If you want things to fall into place and be easy, let them be easy. How? By showing up every day, tuning in, listening for that inner guidance, and acting on it. Following the flow. Trusting your gut.

Doing what feels good (doing good always attracts more good).

People asking me how I made money online was a sign. It was a little clue from the universe that I was meant to be going big on this stuff. I ignored it for a long time. I would give vague answers to questions in comments, but never did a full-on post, email or program on the subject because I didn't think that people would care. But they did care. They wanted it. And apparently, so did I. When I eventually took action on this, and started talking more and more about blogging, and how to make money doing it, the more money I, myself, started making from my blog. Imagine that! If only I had noticed (and acted on) that sign sooner...

When you trust your gut, and you pay attention to the signs you're given, acting on them is only one piece of the puzzle. It's a big piece, but not the only piece. You need confirmation. Confirmation makes you feel good, and like you made the right decision, which will allow you to trust your gut more and open you up to paying closet attention to the signs you're given.

For me, the confirmation I had around writing about how to make money blogging, is having people thanking me for those posts and emails. It was the sign-ups for my Money Making Mama program. It was the gratitude for that program and the inquiries into when I'd be releasing another one. These were all confirmation that I'd made the right decision, that I did the right things, that I was on the right track.

It gave me the confidence to keep going with this work. It motivated me to continue talking about this stuff that really makes me happy and excited.

And now here I am today - doing it! I'm doing what I love, writing to YOU about how you can get paid to be you and do what you truly adore. I'd say noticing, and acting on, that one intuitive nudge to write about making money blogging was a pretty smart move, huh?

What intuitive nudges are you getting right now? What do you know you're meant to be doing? What feels REALLY good to you, and how can you do more of it?

It's time to get out of the cage you've locked yourself in, set your soul free, and live the life of your dreams, now. It's time. You down?

CHAPTER 5

THE POWER OF INVESTING IN YOURSELF

Following your gut is a critical part to success. In fact, I believe it's one of the most important pieces of the Success Puzzle that is often missed. That said, something else that is critical, that is also often missed, is investing in yourself.

This includes investing in your education, your health & wellness, and your up-leveling.

When I first got into coaching, the very first thing I did was hire a private coach. This was a woman I felt a connection with, and who had the experience of growing a successful online coaching business. I wanted to learn from her because I resonated with her and her story, and also because I knew that I couldn't do it all alone. I knew that I needed to get support.

Truth be told, I didn't know a damn thing about coaching when I first got involved with it a few years ago. I knew how to make money online, which is what I was teaching people how to do, but I didn't understand the coaching world or how to perform within it. That's exactly why I hired a coach.

It's kind of funny how I found her, actually. I remember thinking to myself, once I decided to get into coaching, "I need someone to teach me how to monetize this quicker than I could do it on my own", and then I just hit up Google for "business coaches". Ha! That didn't help, though. So I snooped around on Facebook and I found her! I read all of her content, watched her videos, immersed myself in her world and I felt us click. I don't even know how to explain the feeling I had, except that it was very clear that I needed to take immediate action and not second-guess it.

Reaching out to her was the natural next move, and she invited me to get on the phone with her to discuss working together and what that could look like. Uh, yes please! I was so proud of myself for taking action, even though it was messy, and I was just kind of following the flow and "guessing" on my next move, based on how excited I was about it. I was definitely excited about the possibility of working privately with a coach who was where I wanted to be!

I got on the phone with her for our "discovery session", where she talked to me about her process, I told her what I wanted to do, and then I just asked her "how do I pay?". I didn't need to think about it. I was already sold on her, her energy, and her experience. I wanted to learn from the best and I saw her as it. Done and done!

It was important to me to find a coach that could help me get to where I wanted to go with this new business venture. Even though I'd made 6-figures in my couponing/blogging business, it took me years to learn how to do that. I didn't want to spend another many years learning how to do it in my coaching business. I wanted to do it quickly. Hiring a coach to help me shorten the learning curve and shave years off my Money-Making Coach adventure was a no-brainer. I was willing to Pay to Play and it was SO worth it.

Before I hired my first coach, I was scared shitless, and truly, I didn't actually have the money to hire her (I was wiling to put it on a credit card though - I knew it would be worth it - so that wasn't an issue for me… it was still scary), but I knew in my gut that she was the right person. I could feel it when I spoke to her, when I read her content, when I even THOUGHT about the possibility of us working together one-on-one. I just KNEW.

What's important to understand when hiring your next coach (or doing anything, really) is that it's okay, and it's totally normal, to have those feelings of fear and to be terrified to do something big like spend thousands (and in many cases, tens of thousands) of dollars to work with one person. I'd honestly be concerned if you your stomach DIDN'T have butterflies before making a big investment like that!

As long as your gut says HELL YES, you're good.

As long as your soul says DO IT NOW, you're good.

As long as you feel it deep inside of you that YES YES YES, this is what you need to do, you're good.

Make the leap. Do the scary thing. Put yourself out there and lay it all on the line. You're worth it.

Fear is there, present in your life, to try and scare you into submission. To keep you playing safe. To try and keep you from going to that next level that you're craving. Fuck the fear. Do what you know will serve you, no matter how scary it is.

I hired my coach specifically to teach me about marketing in the coaching industry. What I didn't expect was her to talk to me every week about my mindset. I actually tried to ignore that stuff, and patiently wait for her to stop talking about it so she would get to the "good stuff" (the marketing and selling)! I had no idea what I had just got myself into…

I never did the mindset work she told me to do. Not until the last of the 6 months we work together when I finally agreed to give it a try, after months of success at making money, but feeling burnt out and like I could never grow without a different approach. The next week when we met for our weekly phone chat, I confessed that it had worked. She was right. The mindset stuff wasn't bullshit.

It's not easy for me to admit when I'm wrong, but I was most definitely wrong about that. Dismissing mindset work is the biggest mistake I've made in my coaching business thus far. If I had just done the work right away, I'd have accelerated my business even faster, and I wouldn't have got to the point where I was working almost 24/7 (something I was trying to get away from), completely detached from life and loved ones.

Lesson learned!

I resisted mindset work for so long, but when I finally let my guard down and just trusted the process, everything started to fall into place perfectly. It was as someone had waved a magic wand in front of me and changed my life - it happened THAT quickly.

Fast forward a few years and all of the coaches I work with are teaching me about mindset even more than they are about anything else. It's the key focus of my business (and life!), so it's important to me that the people I work with feel this way as well, and have this as the foundation of our work together.

One piece of mindset work that has had the biggest, most significant impact on my life and business is journaling.

I'm never not journaling. It's THE most important piece of "work" I do each and every day. So much so that I often do it multiple times through the day.

Journaling is not like writing in a diary, talking all about what you did that day (like I initially thought it would be), but instead, it's what allows you to create your reality. My journaling process looks like this:

BRAIN DUMP: As soon as I sit down to start journaling, the first course of action is to just write. I release everything from my brain onto paper. I just get it all out of my head, even if it doesn't seem to make sense as it comes out. Release, release, release.

INTENTION OR QUESTION: Once I feel complete, and that everything has been released from my mind, I let my mind wander and see if there's something I want to ask my higher self/the universe or an intention I want to set. If there is, I will write it down. Whenever I have a question come up, I go through a process of essentially coaching myself through it. It's pretty interesting (and super helpful).

DREAM LIFE AFFIRMING: The end of my journaling session is when I go deep into dream life creation. This is how I've manifested almost everything I desire into my life. Simple affirmations around what I want, writing them as though they are already a DONE FREAKIN' DEAL. Like this:

- I love my life, and it just keeps getting better!
- I receive thousands of dollars every day, on repeat.
- My body looks and feels amazing.
- I am super healthy.
- I am super rich.
- I have amazing, supportive, high-vibe friends.
- My clients come to ME and ask to hire me.
- My clients recommend me to everyone they know.
- I am high-vibe and positive, always.
- I hit my money goals again and again. I am a pro at making money!
- Selling comes so naturally to me.
- I have a super hot relationship with my husband.
- My kids are happy, health, respectful, and the best of friends.
- I create my own reality.
- I am a VIP!
- I always get free upgrades and bonuses.
- Everything is always perfect for me.

And so on and so forth!

Honestly, journaling is the best thing I've ever done. It changes my vibe instantly, gets me in flow, and brings me back to the core of what I'm here to do: impact millions, change lives and create a high-vibe, VIP lifestyle for myself and my family.

Journaling is a game-changer. If you haven't done it, or if you have but not consistently, give it a go. It's the secret sauce to my success. I only wish I had known about its powers sooner! Now, if I don't journal first thing in the morning, I feel naked as I go throughout my day. I feel angry, frustrated, and lost. It's not until I sit down and journal my thoughts, call in my dream life, and affirm my desires, that I raise my vibe and feel incredible. Only then am I truly ready to start my day and get to action.

Showing up and doing your mindset work is a daily must-do. It's not something you can skip.

You can do all the "work" you want:

- Create sales pages
- Launch new offers
- Write copy
- Deliver value
- Interact with your community
- Sell and sell some more
- Set up the email sequence
- Do the advertising
- Pitch your services/products

And you WILL make money, you WILL help people, you WILL be successful in the eyes of others, but -

It won't feel good. Not long term, anyway. Eventually, what will happen, is you will end up feeling overworked, overwhelmed and ready to punch someone in the face just for looking at you at the wrong way. Your energy will off. You will resent your clients, resent your work, and wonder why the hell you even started this business in the first place.

Because although your business actions are on point, you're doing the WORK, you're crossing your T's and dotting your I's, you won't feel completely fulfilled. Something will be missing. That something will make itself apparent in your journaling. And when it does, you can take action on it and completely transform your life.

Mindset work isn't just about journaling (although I truly believe that it's the #1 way to create what you want in your life). There are many different things you can do that would fall under the category of mindset work. Things that have the power to completely change your life for the better and have an incredible effect on what you're able to be, do and have in your life.

MEDITATION (even for just a few minutes a day) is one thing you can do.

VISUALIZATION is another (visualizing what you want to be, do and have, as if it's already your reality).

FEELING the feelings of already having the thing/experience that you want is one more.

And many more, still, of course. I'm not an expert on mindset work. What I am, though, is someone who passionately pursues it and recommends it! Journaling alone has changed my life in so many ways, in just a few short years. I've been able to manifest so much through journaling. I'm actually appalled (and truly confused) when someone, especially someone in business, tells me that they don't journal. Jaw to the floor. But then I get to talk about how to use it to change your world, and it makes me feel so good to share this tiny action with people.

(A tiny action that has the potential to rock your freakin' world, by the way - in case you didn't get that by now!)

Mindset work is the most important thing I learned through working with multiple coaches over the years, but in addition to that, I learn a heap of other things that I wouldn't have been able to learn on my own (well, I could have, but it would have taken me years of learning, trying, failing, trying again... until I got it right).

I learned all about how to write to sell, how to magnetize people to me and get them EXCITED about working with me. I learned how to create content all day, every day, how to engage with my audience, and how to sell all day long, while still having a life. (I honestly just "work" a few hours a day, maximum. The rest of the day, I relax, hang out, have fun, and just do whatever the hell I want to do.

I discovered how to sell ME, in a way that was easy, fun, and that didn't feel like "work" at all.

There's no way I could have done this all on my own. If I had never hired my first coach, and the many coaches after her (not to mention programs, events, and trainings), I would likely still be flailing around, guessing my way through life instead of having someone tell me exactly how to do it in a way that didn't feel forced and would get me phenomenal results. I'm so grateful that I found coaching and for the support my coaches over the years have given me. I wouldn't be where I am today if it weren't for them.

Simply put, investing in yourself, and learning what you need to learn (whether that's mindset work, sales strategies, or how to write better so that people are magnetized to you and your work), is one of the most important (and beneficial) things you can do for yourself. Don't skimp on it.

What can you do today, this week, or this month, to invest in yourself and get the support you need? How will you know if a coach is a HELL YES for you? Define that now so you'll know it when you feel it.

And then? Make the leap. Do it for you. Yes, you are ready. No you don't need to do ___ first or have ___ first. Now is the only time. Now is THE time.

It's time to jump. I'll see ya on the other side!

CHAPTER 6

TOP TEN MINDSET SHIFTS I HAD TO MAKE TO TAKE MY BUSINESS TO THE NEXT LEVEL

Over the course of the 14+ years I've been building and growing businesses online, I've discovered that of ALL the money I've made, very little of it actually came from the strategy of "making money".

Where it actually came from is from changing my mindset.

I've learned a lot of over the past 3 (almost 4 at this point) years around mindset and how having a good one plays a huge role in your business and life, but the biggest thing I learned was this:

What you think about is what you will create.

So all of the debt you have? That's on you. It happened because of thoughts and beliefs that you had in the past, which influenced your behaviours that let you to incur this debt.

The bad relationships you were in? That's on you, too. Those happened because of, again, the thoughts and beliefs that you had in the past, which influenced your behaviours that led you to meeting, and getting into a relationship with these totally-wrong-for-you people.

And of course, where you are right now, in business, in life, in everything… yep, also on you. Also because of the behaviours that came from your thoughts and beliefs.

Once I learned this, I was, first and foremost, pissed at myself for not knowing this sooner, but then grateful. Grateful for the knowledge I now had that would allow me to radically change my life for the better.

I felt FREE.

I knew that it was all on me now (just as it has always been, but what I didn't know up until that point), and knew that if I wanted my life, or certain areas of my life, to change and improve, I needed to change my thoughts and beliefs.

At which point, my behaviours would change and as such, my results and experiences would change.

It's like freakin' magic, this mindset stuff, I tell ya!

I can't believe that, for so long, I actually made fun of people who did this work, who believed in something greater themselves.

On the surface, I believed they were weird and "too spiritual", but deep down, I was jealous that their life always seemed to work out for them.

Now here I am walking around, saging my house, meditating while talking to the universe, and using tarot cards like I'm some kind of psychic on a mission to make magic everywhere (I am).

So, looks like I maybe was wrong about those "weird, ultra

spiritual" people. Ha!

The main reason I didn't understand the whole "mindset stuff" is because, honestly, I just didn't understand it.

It was weird to me because I didn't get it. Didn't know how to apply it to my life. Didn't know how to ignore the "practical" side of my brain that told me "this isn't how the world works" and just BELIEVE.

It took a long time, thousands of dollars on mentors and trainings and books and workshops that taught me most of what I know today.

Not to mention all of the stress, all of the overwhelm, all of the uncertainties, and all of the moments I lie on the floor, crying my eyes out, begging it to work.

Scared shitless that I would end up broke if I kept up what I was doing, yet still truly believing this was the only way.

Pushing harder and harder every day, trying so fucking hard to get past the fears, to believe, believe, believe and trust that everything was working out for me.

There were many times I would just crack.

Spend the day in my bed, hiding from my family, pretending I was sick, when really I was too embarrassed to tell them I was running out of money fast, and I was scared.

Feeling like a failure.

Feeling like I was crazy.

Feeling like a terrible mom, wide, friend, mentor, PERSON.

"Please just work! I can't take this anymore!", I'd cry out, to who, I don't know, but hoping someone, somewhere would hear me and help me the fuck out.

They didn't.

I was repeatedly thrown to the ground, time and time again, left bruised and bloody, oftentimes blacking out completely and waking up in a world of pain.

But every time -

Every motherfucking time -

I would GET BACK UP and eventually I just screamed (at the top of my lungs in my bedroom one day) -

"I give the fuck up. I'm done. I don't damn well care anymore. I'm gonna do what I want and it's gonna work, and that's just the way it is. Enough is enough of this bullshit. Fuck it all."

And then I got the fuck up.

And I ran this bitch the way I've always wanted to, with the belief in the background, always, that this was gonna work. It was going to work. IT WAS GOING TO WORK.

It was slow.

It was painful.

But I never gave up because I knew. I just knew. This is what I needed.

That beating? Needed it.

That breakdown? Needed it.

And today?

Well...

Today is fucking fabulous, I'm doing what I want, and yep... you guessed it... it's working.

I get paid to be me.

People love to pay me and often tell me this in conversation.

All I have to do, ever, is show up and do whatever I want to do. Nothing more, nothing less.

I can say what I want, do what I want, be who I AM, and the money rolls in, on repeat, day after day.

I'd say I'm surprised, but I'm not. This is how it was always supposed to be.

All of this to say:

You know what's right for you. You know what you're meant to do, and how it's all meant to BE.

So why are you settling?

Why are you allowing yourself to give up and quit (or at least consider it) when things get a bit challenging?

Know this, believe this, trust this:

You can have it all, on your terms, right now, but it ain't gonna happen until you decide that you will accept nothing less.

That's the work. The mindset work that works. The only thing that matters.

So with that said, here are the top 10 mindset shifts that I had to make, in order to take my business (and my life) to the next level:

1. Do what you want. *(Fuck the rules)*

Holy shit, this is my favorite one of all. If I had just realized this years ago, my life would be so different.

The truth is, the way YOU want to do things, is the actual RIGHT way to do things because it all just flows and feels easy.

When things feel easy, you tend to want to keep doing them, put in the effort, and get better and better.

I started to believe that didn't have to do what everyone else was doing and could totally just make up my own rules and do what I please. Once that belief was ingrained, my business blew up (in a good way) and my life changed forever.

2. The nudges don't lie.

I didn't want to believe it in the past (it was too "weird" for me back then), but I have always received "signs" and "gut feelings" (we all do, whether we choose to acknowledge them or not) about certain situations.

Way back, I would often ignore them, believing they were just a "coincidence".

These days though, as my spiritual practice evolves, I've learned that those nudges? They don't lie and you'd better follow them.

3. The physical feel-good feelings are what matter most.

One of the biggest shifts I've made is actually more of a physical than mental shift, and that is the feel-good-feelings, and acting on those.

The biggest way I make decisions now, is based on how I feel - physically.

When something is the right decision, I physically feel good. My body is buzzing, I get butterflies in my stomach, and I have this force of energy that is so powerful I can hardly sit still.

When something ISN'T the right decision, well, I feel the opposite of that. Or I feel nothing at all.

The next time you need to make a decision about something,

tune in to how you're feeling - physically - before deciding.

4. It's never about the money.

I used to do things because I knew they would make me money, not because I actually wanted to do them.

I was so caught up in this negative, scarcity energy of "I need to make a lot of money, and I need to make it now" that I let that rule me and the actions I would take each day.

It wasn't until I made that decision to do what I want to do, the way I want to do it, that I realized it's not about the money at all. It's never about the money. The money is NOT what I want.

My deep desire is ultimately to change the world with my words and actions. To show others what's possible for them. To inspire millions of people around the world to do what they love, and to stop settling for a life they aren't madly in love with.

It was never about the money. So why was I making that my focus?

Once I realized this, and shifted my beliefs and actions, to incorporate the IMPACT I wanted to make, everything changed.

(And the cool thing? My income increased, too.)

5. Let it be easy.

I made everything hard for so long. I truly thought that in order for me to have and experience the success I wanted, I would have to "work hard", and then it was a matter of how hard I could work.

I'd sacrifice sleep all the time, I'd ditch my friends and family to work, I gave up exercise so I could have more time work on my business and making money...

Life was no longer enjoyable, honestly. Even though I LOVED my work and really did love doing it, I didn't love the fact that in order for me to do it, I had to ALWAYS do it, and sacrifice other things and people that I cared about.

Another mindset shift I had to make: This shit gets to be easy.

And just like that, again, everything changed. The easier I allowed things to be, the easier they became.

6. Everything always works out for me.

When I look back at the "bad" moments in my life - the times when everything felt hard and like the world was out to get me - the moments when I truly thought "this is it, this is when it all goes to shit" -

That's when everything turns around and magic happens for me.

This is the case every single time, with every single negative experience in my life. It all worked out for me, in my favor, again and again.

Now, I choose to believe that everything always works out for me, even if it feels like it isn't. Especially when it feels like it isn't.

And then it does. Like always.

7. The breakthrough is in the breakdown.

I used to be deathly afraid of bad stuff happening in my life. I was constantly worried about bad days, bad people, bad experiences, and it ruled my freakin' life.

Yet, of course, as is life, breakdowns always did happen. Not often, thankfully, but they did, and they will continue too.

The interesting thing I noticed when I looked back on these times from the past, I realized that all of my big, best ideas came from those moments.

My big breakthrough moments absolutely came immediately after a massive breakdowns.

8. Abundance is a state of mind.

It really, truly is. Abundance is not money in the bank. It's not stuff in your house or garage.

This is honestly one of the biggest lessons I've ever learned in my life, and what has allowed me to manifest a flood of money, soulmate friends and clients, experiences, and on occasion, stuff, into my life, super fast and with total ease.

It wasn't until I changed my thinking on what abundance actually meant to me, that I actually started to experience true abundance in my life.

9. I am worthy and I am enough.

Do you ever think about something and get that annoying voice that pops into your head and asks "who do you think you are to want that?"?

Yeah. That's what I'm talking about here. This is the mindset shift that had such a profound effect on me, that once I really took to it and truly believed it, opportunities started to fall into my lap, often with zero effort on my part.

I decided that I was going to stop hindering myself and holding myself back by accepting the incorrect thought that I wasn't worthy enough to have what I wanted, and instead would choose to accept myself as worthy and enough.

Of all of the mindset shifts I'm mentioning here, this is the one that was the hardest for me to make. It was hard. I continually fought myself on it. I still do sometimes.

But things are different than they were even a year ago in the sense that I know my worth. And I choose, over and over, day after day, to hold that in my mind and believe it.

10. You get what you believe is possible. (Hint: It's ALL possible.)

If you want to change your life for the better, forever and ever, over and over again, this is the number one mindset shift that I recommend you make.

This is what changed everything for me. Everything.

Once I dropped the BS beliefs I had around receiving and changed them to beliefs I WANTED to have, my world was rocked in the best way possible.

Believe I can get paid just to be me? Yep. (And do it is.)

Believe that I can work from anywhere in the world? Yep. (And so it is.)

Believe that I can drive a super sexy car and live in my favorite neighborbood? Yep. (And so it is.)

I believed it was possible for me, and then it happened. Just like that.

(See, I told you it's like magic!)

What I've really learned through this process of changing my beliefs, upgrade my mindset and creating the life of my dreams, through and through, is that I'm the one in charge here.

No one gets to tell me what to think, or say, or do, or believe.

That's on me.

And it's on you, too.

Everything you want, is possible for you, it's meant for you, it's ready for you now, and all you've gotta do to call it yours?

Is believe that it already is.

Is it time to upgrade your mindset? Better get on it. Everything you've ever wanted is waiting for you.

No pressure..

CHAPTER 7

YOU GET TO DO IT **YOUR** WAY

A year or so into my business, I was working mostly with one-on-one clients, and doing a handful of group programs here and there. I didn't know another way to do it. I just knew that I wanted to work with women to help them with their online business, so I did what I knew to do.

Even though it was slowly killing me.

I loved it, but I was exhausted.

It takes a ton of mental energy to mentor other people, to go deep into their stories and help them, which always left me feeling tired and ready to crash at the end of the day. I barely had any time left over for my family or friends - or even myself. After a full day of client calls I just wanted to crawl into bed and go to sleep!

At the end of the day, my brain was absolute mush. I couldn't hold a conversation. I could barely keep my eyes open!

I knew I'd have to sacrifice sleep sometimes. I knew that being tired occasionally was part of the deal. I just didn't expect so much of it! I was finding it harder and harder to believe that I could do this much longer.

As much as I loved working with my clients, I just didn't want to work with a ton of them at once, and I definitely didn't want to be on the phone all day long!

I was learning some pretty serious lessons around acceptance and a clear understanding of what I truly wanted my days and life to look like. And it wasn't like this…

I'd built up a list of clients that I loved working with (learning who I DIDN'T love working with in the process!), learned how to run a successful coaching program, both privately and in group format, I'd learned and practiced my coaching skills for over a year, I was getting better and better, everything was going well, except…

My sanity took a bit of a hit. A massive hit, in fact.

I was running on an empty tank most of the time. I was never able to operate at full capacity because I just didn't have the energy. I wasn't able to drop the struggle. I never had a chance to breathe!

I knew I didn't want to only be doing just one-on-one coaching calls with my clients, they were taking up so much of my time each day (an hour each, in most cases). It was too much and things needed to change if I was ever going to feel good about this business I'd built and truly reap the rewards of it.

The rewards that people always complimented me on, not fully understanding the amount of effort that was required for me to attain those rewards.

See, on the outside, it looked like I had it all. I'd made $250,000 in the very first year of a brand new business, and to make that, all I had to do was talk about my favorite things ever: business and money.

People commented all of the time that I was "so lucky". That it must be nice to have "so much" free time to spend my days doing and talking about what I wanted. Ha! If they only knew...

I was always tired.

I was spending more money than I was receiving.

I was resentful of my quick success.

As grateful as I am for it all, and as fun as a lot of parts of it were, I was not happy. It was a rough first year. I was ready for life to be easy.

I knew it was time to shake things up. Starting with taking back some of my time by diversifying my income.

Although, at the time, I didn't realize that diversifying my income was something that I needed to do. I just knew that something had to change. I had to find a way to make money without running myself into the ground.

Over the past 14 years of building online business, there's a few things I wish I'd started doing sooner. One of those things is diversifying my income. I would have saved myself years of stress, overwhelm and fear, had I just implemented this one thing early on.

Eventually I did, of course. It's still something I'm working on (and likely something I'll always be working on). I'm nowhere near where I want to be with this habit, but I'm certainly better off now than I was just a few years ago, when I was relying on my income from just ONE source (and freaking the fuck out if it wasn't coming in as quickly as I wanted it to).

I discovered that what really mattered wasn't how much money I was making, but how I felt when the money came in. Making a lot of money didn't matter to me if I wasn't enjoying myself in the process of making it.

Helping others, serving them in a big way and teaching them everything I knew around how to build a successful, profitable online business, was (and is!) my passion - but I will no longer do it at the expense of my own well-being. And that's exactly what I was doing.

I had to shift. I had to change the way I was showing up and how I was doing things in my business each day.

In order for me to truly give myself and my knowledge, I needed to do it in a way that didn't suck all of the energy out of me and didn't require me to spend hours and hours every day doing it.

So, I set out to diversify my income, save a ton of time, and bring sanity back to my life.

I started testing new things, starting with the way I was promoting my offers.

At that point, Facebook groups was my top strategy. I was consistently showing up multiple times every day in other peoples' groups, as well as in my own (but I didn't have my own until around 6 months in). I was spending 12+ hours a day in Facebook group. No, that's not a typo. TWELVE HOURS. Every single day.

Insanity, I know. No wonder I was so damn tired all of the time! But it worked.

People noticed me. They really SAW me. They were magnetized

by my content, sure, but mostly, without a doubt, my work ethic. (If there's one surprising thing I've learned over the past few years it's that if you have an incredible work ethic, people are drawn to you and everything you do - they're so in awe of you and can't look away).

My sales went through the roof. Money was flowing in, over and over. Clients were signing up to work with me left and right.

It's definitely one of the best things I could have done when I first started and even though I was tired as hell, I don't regret it for a second. It taught me so much - including the fact that I don't want to be tired as hell all the time!

In addition to Facebook groups, I was also promoting my offers through email, though not as consistently as I was with Facebook.

That's it, though. That's pretty much all I was doing. Facebook and email.

Diversifying was gonna be easy! I had so many options! At least these were my initial thoughts...

It was a tough start. Facebook groups were everything to me. I was terrified to do something different, with the fear that I would "lose" the successful business that I had built on them alone. But I knew that if was ever doing to reclaim my sanity, I needed to scale back. So I did it, as hard as it felt.

I cut my time on Facebook groups way back, and added new promotional strategies to my arsenal:

- Increasing the frequency I was emailing my list (including scheduling emails when necessary).

- Doing more promotional videos and livestreams on Facebook (and eventually, on Instagram).
- Hosting webinars and selling on those (before I realized I hated them).
- Doing live challenges in my own Facebook group and through email growing my email list AND my group at the same time).
- Reaching out privately to potential clients, instead of waiting for them to come to me (which is hilarious because now they DO come to me and I rarely reach out to them… but I was willing to try anything at the time!).

One of the biggest shifts I made, though, wasn't actually my promotional activities, but in fact, WHAT I was ultimately promoting.

I had to get out of the mindset of "the only way to make money is with one-on-one clients" and into one of "money comes from doing what you truly love and from what feels good". And although I absolutely DID love what I was doing, I didn't love the way that it was going. I didn't love the corner I had put myself in. The corner that was all about doing things one way.

I had to make the conscious decision to tweak the way I did business so that I could free up more of my time and actually live my life doing more than just talking on the phone for hours a day. Letting go of the belief that, in order to hit my money goals, I had to strictly do one-on-one coaching, was my first step.

Then, it was diversifying my income, of course. Starting with changing the way I was doing my promotions/selling.

From there, it was changing what I was selling, so that it was in alignment with how I wanted to show up and what I really wanted to do. No more doing things just because I knew I could make money doing them.

Really, when I look back on it, the biggest shift didn't come from any one thing. It came from all of the 3 things above, combined. Let me recap for you:

STEP 1: Adopt the belief that you can do things YOUR way, and that ultimately you have to do what feels good to you, if you want to be successful and maintain any kind of sanity.

STEP 2: Test out new ways to promote your current offers and to promote yourself. Don't get stuck doing the same thing forever (unless you love it forever, of course).

STEP 3: Decide to only sell things that are in alignment for you, and not what you think you *have* to sell. Stick to that decision. It's a game-changer.

All of these 3 steps are important. They're all necessary.

Take a look at how you're currently showing up in your life and business. Are you left feeling exhausted and tapped out at the end of the day? Do you feel any kind of resentment toward your clients or other people you work with? Do you wake up feeling any kind of dread to do what you need to do that day?

If you answered yes to any of the questions above, bad news:

Your business isn't sustainable and if you're making money, it ain't gonna last.

There is good news, though:

You can change this. Quite easily, actually. How? Make the decision that from this moment forward, you will stop doing things that feel like a burden.

That's it. That's all that's required to completely change things around for the better.

You don't have to keep doing the same thing you've been doing for months or years, even if it's been working ("working" meaning you're getting something out of it, such as money, recognition, etc.). You can change things at a moment's notice and that's that.

If you're feeling overwhelmed, frustrated or just plain TIRED, then you know it's time to make a change.

The only way to make money isn't to do the same thing on repeat, day after day, forever and ever. (Unless that's what lights you up, of course! But I'm willing to guess that it's not.. as most of us tend to get bored if we do the same thing repeatedly.)

The only way to make money isn't to do what everyone else is doing, if it doesn't set your soul on fire.

The only way to make money isn't to work 24/7, constantly glued to your phone and laptop.

There is another way. There are many ways. And they start with doing what you love, yes, but mostly, doing what you love in the WAY you love to do it.

Once I got out of my own way, and truly allowed things to be easy, I started to make money even faster. I brought in $500,000 in my second year of business - and it was easier than ever. I was working less and doing things that I truly loved to do, in the way I loved to do them.

I stopped doing the shit that I hated doing.

I stopped trying to impress others with my work ethic.

I stopped believing that things had to be done a certain way in order to work for me.

And instead, I just followed my flow. I did what felt good, each day, and I stopped doing anything that felt like a chore. I found ways to sell that were fun for me; I actually started to enjoy the art of sales!

Showing up every day, writing, creating, selling, sharing my message.. it was something I actually started to love doing - when previously it felt like something I HAD to do. It's amazing how a slight shift in your beliefs can massively impact your quality of life.

Something you need to know if you're ever gonna be successful in business:

It doesn't work if it doesn't work for YOU. Meaning, of course, that if you don't like what you're doing (or the way you're doing it), aren't enjoying yourself, or doing it makes you feel resentful or negative in any way, then then you will never be successful doing it. If you *do* somehow manage to find success doing the stuff you don't like or enjoy, it will be impossible to hold on to. Ultimately, you will sabotage yourself and your success, because it's not being experienced in a way that makes you come alive.

True success requires you to say the word "no" a lot.

No to what doesn't light you up.

No to what you don't enjoy.

No to what doesn't feel right.

No to what most other people are doing.

No to what doesn't align with your core values.

This means you will piss a lot of people off. A lot of people who want you to do things the way THEY want you to do them. And you will be tempted, because I know you love to make other people happy. Plus, they offered you money to do it! Let me tell you something though...

If you continue to say YES to the things that are really, deep down, a HELL NO, you will continue to push success (and your happiness) away.

So here's what to do, plain and simple:

Practice saying no to what's not aligned for you, so you can start saying yes to what is. It makes all the difference. I promise.

CHAPTER 8

OVERWORKED & OVERWHELMED

To an outsider looking in, I had a hugely successful business. I had consistent clients, my income was increasing month after month, and my visibility and authority was more impressive than it'd ever been.

My life was also more extravagant than it'd ever been, with a team full of people cleaning my house, washing my car, driving me around, picking out my clothes, doing my make-up, following me around like paparazzi.

I was happily married, with two amazing kids that kept me on my toes, living in a beautiful home and driving a luxury vehicle (the one I'd wanted for over a decade but had convinced myself I'd never be able to afford).

Everything was incredible.

Everything was exactly as I'd always wanted.

And to everyone around me, everything was perfect.

THE PROBLEM WITH PERFECTION

There was just one problem: I was tired. Really freakin' tired. So tired that I was napping at any chance I got, barely able to function throughout the day, completely shut off from the world, living in my own head (and online).

I was working with dozens of private clients at a time, taking on anyone, at any price point, just to prove that I could... and, if I'm being honest, because I was scared that if I DIDN'T continue saying YES to clients who wanted to work with me, the money would dry up, and I'd be broke again.

The scarcity mindset that I possessed was insane. I'd celebrate every dollar that I made, and then, as soon as I made it, I'd immediately get worried about where the next dollar would come from. I lived constantly with the fear that signing on a new client or selling a spot in one of my programs was just a fluke (as everyone around me tried to convince me of).

So I said yes, over and over again, to anyone who inquired about working together. YES, I can work out a package for you. YES, I have space available. YES, you can have a discount. YES, I can give you this extra thing and that extra thing as a bonus. Of course! Just pretty please say YES to me. Pretty please pay me.

As much as I knew how to help my clients with what they were paying me to help them with, many of my clients in the beginning were not a good fit. They were hesitant to do the work, because they were looking for a magic pill to help them. They were scared and not go-getters, like me.

But I said yes. To everyone (with the exception of maybe one person).

And I made money. A LOT of money. It wasn't even hard. What it was, though, was exhausting, frustrating, and overwhelming. It's not that I hated my clients, it's that I hated what my life had turned into, which was a 24/7 machine that never stopped.

THE DAY MY BODY TRIED TO KILL ME

After months and months of overworking myself, completely maxed out and frustrated, things changed.

My body had had enough of me putting it through the ringer, and it tried to kill me.

Around midnight on a Tuesday (just kidding...I don't know what day of the week it was!), I woke up in a state of panic. Everyone in the house was sleeping, and I was freaking out. About what, I don't know, but my body was going batshit crazy. All of a sudden, my entire body went numb, and I felt like I couldn't breathe.

The air was thick. It was getting harder and harder to take it in. I felt like someone was sitting on my chest.

I lay there for a few minutes and thought about what I should do. Should I just try to calm myself down and go back to sleep? Should I wake up Richard (who was fast asleep beside me)? Should I get checked out by a doctor? Am I really dying right now?

The thought of going to the hospital made me want to puke. Sitting in a waiting room for hours, all alone? I already hated hospitals to begin with… ugh.

I tried to shake it off, to coach myself to just breathe, to relax, to calm my anxiety.

But it wasn't working. In fact, it was making things worse. Much worse. My heart was beating so fast, I thought it was gonna be the death of me.

I quickly got dressed and called 911, told them I couldn't breathe and felt like someone was repeatedly stabbing me with a million knives in my chest. Then I sat on the porch while waiting for them to arrive.

A few minutes later, I heard sirens getting closer and closer, and the next thing I knew, the ambulance was at my front door. The paramedics jumped out and ran over to me to see what was happening.

Long story short, they told me to chill the fuck out, breathe, and I'd be fine, but I didn't believe them and made them take me to the hospital. Once a boss, always a boss…what can I say? They rolled their eyes and put me on a stretcher in the back of the ambulance.

When I was eventually seen by a doctor (after lying on a stretcher in the hallway for hours—yay for free healthcare), he asked me to explain what'd been going on before this freak-out—which, by this point, had subsided—happened.

I explained that I wasn't sleeping much because I had started a new business and was working really hard on growing it quickly, so I was spending a lot of time on it.

I spoke honestly about what my day looked like: glued to my computer practically 24/7, anxiety and fear through the roof, working, working, and working some more, trying to prove myself to everyone around me (including my own ego) that I could do it.

The doctor nicely told me, just like the paramedics, to chill the fuck out and stop being a workaholic. He explained that I'd just had a mini panic attack and that in order to avoid something like that happening again, I needed to bring more serenity and calm into my life.

I laughed. "I don't know what that even means," I said. I think he thought I was kidding, because he laughed back and told me to have a good rest of my night.

He sent me home with a tiny little anti-anxiety pill, and I never saw him again. (Thankfully.)

MY WAKE-UP MOMENT

This was my wake-up call. This was that moment for me when I realized that if I didn't change the way I was living my life and running my business, I would likely die from a heart attack, over-exertion, or some other form of "death by constant hustle" activity.

I've always been a hard worker, and I do love being that way. I ADORE the hustle, and it's a big part of my life. One that I'll never be willing to let go of. Yet, at the same time, I also know how important it is to take time to just BE.

You don't have to constantly be hustling in order to grow your business. You don't need to work 24/7 just to pay the bills.

The hustle doesn't mean never turning off your computer.

The hustle doesn't mean that you can't ever take an hour away from "working".

The hustle doesn't mean that you aren't allowed to sleep.

The hustle is doing what you LOVE to do, and doing a lot of it, so long as it continues to feel easy and joyful.

Life is meant to be lived and enjoyed, and at the time of my panic attack, I was definitely not living my life to the fullest, nor was I enjoying it very much, quite honestly!

Even though I had money, I had consistent paying clients who wanted to work with me, I had a large following online, I was travelling business class around the world...

I wasn't happy.

In fact, I was just as depressed as I was when I was broke.

All because I didn't know how to actually love my life NOW, instead of taking what I already had for granted, and always chasing something more, something bigger, something supposedly "better".

How Saying HELL NO Brought More HELL YES into My Life

In an effort to start loving my life, I started to work less. I still busted my ass, don't get me wrong, but I did so on the stuff that mattered. I did so on the stuff that would actually make a difference, and I ignored everything else.

I also started saying NO a lot more.

No to clients that I knew weren't a good fit.

No to people asking me to be a part of their online summit.

No to strangers begging to "pick my brain".

The funny thing is, the more I said NO, the more that YES opportunities came my way. I was able to more easily identify and agree to HELL YES opportunities because I made space for them by letting go of the HELL NO opportunities. Huh. Imagine that!

This was another big a-ha moment for me that changed the way I showed up, lived my life, and ran my business.

I started consistently saying "no" to anything that wasn't an easy "hell yes". No more "I need to think about it" or "I'm not sure" or "Maybe"... It's either HELL YES or it's HELL NO. Straight up. No question.

This is one of those "tips" that has the ability to change your life for-freakin'-ever, if you actually commit to it. It certainly changed mine, and it's something I'm always teaching my clients, because if there's anything I've learned over the past decade plus of building online businesses, it's that hesitation is a money-killer. A success-killer.

The longer you wait to make a decision, the harder the decision becomes to make, which means that you're likely to miss out on opportunities that could potentially serve you in a big way.

Commit to the decision. Yes. Or no. What's it gonna be? Just decide.

So the lesson here, for me and for you, is that it's okay to take a step back, evaluate what you're doing, and determine whether or not it's working for you.

If you're constantly feeling overwhelmed and frazzled, then what you're doing isn't working.

If you're not having fun, then what you're doing isn't working.

If you're worried all of the time, totally stressed to the max, then what you're doing isn't working.

It's completely fine to take a break when you need it; to walk away and take the time to breathe and just BE, so that you can come back refreshed and ready to manifest the fuck out of what you want in life (and do the work to get it).

The world won't end if you're not online for an hour, or if you forget your phone at home for the afternoon while you're out with your family. The internet will survive without you. I promise.

I should mention that when I say "take a break", I don't mean that you should completely disappear for weeks at a time. If you can do that, you're not an entrepreneur who's madly in love with what she does, and you're never gonna make it (doing that one thing, anyway).

You can't just go rogue.

Take a break, sure! Just don't fuck off all together, unless you want to be completely forgotten.

There are billions of people in the world, and if you're not there for your audience, there will be someone else who is—and that's who they'll remember. Not you.

So take a day off, ignore the world, do your thing, but then?

Come back, show up, give us all of you, and resume your regular daily activities.

There's nothing more important than your health, so take care of yourself, and then you'll be better equipped to show up fully for your audience and provide them with the support and guidance that they need each day.

You don't have to work 24/7 in order to hit your goals. You're allowed to sleep. You're allowed to put the phone away for a few hours. You're allowed to eat a meal without photographing it first.

You can do things your way, and you have the freedom to have "your way" look any way you damn well please.

A common belief that I hear all the time in business, is this:

"The harder I work, the more money I make."

Here's the truth: that's a straight-up lie, and you can go right ahead and ignore it.

I've found that the less I work, the more money I make. I mean yeah, sure, I've still gotta do the work. I've still gotta hustle my ass off if I want something. I can't just meditate, cross my fingers and get what I want magically landing in my lap. Ain't gonna happen.

That being said, the most profitable months in my business are not the months that I worked the hardest or put in the most hours.

The most profitable months in my business are the months when I'm off doing fun shit, like travelling, hosting events, buying myself something I've wanted for a long while (this year it was my new car!), or spending more time with friends and family.

What I've discovered is that the money flows when I feel calm, relaxed, at ease…not when I'm running around with a million to-do's on my calendar. Fuck that noise anyway. Who actually wants that?

You didn't start this business as a replacement for your 9-5, where you have to constantly hustle, never sleep, constantly go go go, round and round, in circles.

You started this business to have the freedom to do what you want, when you want, how you want, without the struggle. So then, how does that work?

Not by working your ass off all day, every day, that's for sure.

You've gotta work, YES.

You've gotta commit, YES.

You've gotta be hungry for what you want, YES.

You've gotta hustle, YES.

You've gotta be persistent, YES.

But also? You've gotta LIVE.

From one workaholic to another, please don't forget to live, okay?

You are worthy of a lifetime of bliss, of joy, of abundance, of freedom, without working yourself into the ground to get it. Don't ever forget that.

CHAPTER 9

HUSTLE LOVER

Over more than a decade spent building businesses online (along with a lifetime of being an entrepreneur), I've come to realize that there are two types of people.

There are those who believe that the word "hustle" is good and those who believe that the word "hustle" is bad.

The belief is this: you either must work 24/7 to find success or you must work as little as possible to find success.

You know what?

Both people are right.

How can that be?

Simply put: you get to choose what you believe, and what you believe becomes your reality.

What Does "Hustle" Mean to You?

If, deep down, you believe that the word "hustle" means you must work 24/7 to get what you want, then that will be your experience.

If, on the other hand, you believe that the word "hustle" just means living your life, then all you will ever have to do to get what you want is live your life.

See what I mean?

It's a conscious decision around what meaning you, personally, are giving to the word "hustle".

It's been a heated argument online for years now, and likely always will be. There's the pro-hustle camp and there's the anti-hustle camp, and the two just can't get along.

(Which is a shame, because imagine how amazing the world would be if we all just got along. But I digress...)

There is a lot of stigma around the *word* "hustle" and around the *action* of hustle. There are people who love it and people who hate it, and very few people in between.

I've seen communities built on all ease and no hustle (which is technically impossible—to be successful without any kind of hustle, I mean), and I've seen communities that are all "it's supposed to be hard, so suck it up and get to work"—a.k.a. all hustle and no ease.

I'm in the middle of both camps.

The hustle is necessary. The feeling you attach to the hustle is what will make it either a fun and enjoyable experience or one that feels like you were just told you have to chop onions in the back of a restaurant for ten hours a day.

Don't let anyone trick you into believing that you can grow a thriving business without lifting a finger, because it just isn't possible.

You've gotta work.

You've gotta put in the time.

You've gotta show up.

No one is going to do the work for you, and the work must be done.

That means, of course, that it's all on you, sister!

You need to own it, and get it done.

When "Hustle" Really Means "Play"

Good news, though; the hustle? It can actually feel like play time.

I believe that the hustle is easy. In fact, I find ease WITHIN the hustle.

This is what "the hustle" means to me:

- The hustle means writing about things I'm excited to share.
- The hustle means selling things I'm passionate about.
- The hustle means showing behind-the-scenes of my life and business.
- The hustle means writing in my journal.
- The hustle means tracking my income, expenses, and all money stuff.
- The hustle means acting from a place of flow and ease (letting the hustle be easy).
- The hustle means showing up, day after day, sharing what's on my heart.
- The hustle means spending time with friends and family.
- The hustle means travelling and experiencing new things in new places.
- The hustle means reading and learning every day.
- The hustle means hanging out with my community online.

- The hustle means telling people what I'm doing and sharing my experiences.
- The hustle means talking about lessons I've learned and being an open book with my audience.
- The hustle means living my life.

When the majority of people hear the word "hustle", what they're really hearing is constant work, no breaks, and insane amounts of sacrifice.

There is a huge collective belief that "hustle" means you're repeatedly working your ass off, day in and day out, and that's simply not true.

I'm here to set the record straight.

"Hustle" really means to "do".

What, exactly, you're doing is up to you—it won't look the same for you as it does for me, and vice versa.

Therefore, the hustle could mean writing a blog post. It could also mean baking a cake or travelling from one location to another.

The hustle could mean shooting a video and sharing it online. Or, it could mean doing a photoshoot for your new website.

What the hustle tasks actually are is completely up to you.

In truth, the hustle is life. It's you LIVING your life.

It doesn't have to mean long days, with you being glued to your laptop 24/7, or doing shit you hate, unless you want it to.

It means whatever you want it to mean.

Let me be clear on one thing:

I'm a firm believer in hard work.

I don't believe that you can sit around, do nothing except watch Netflix all day, and be successful.

I really don't.

I think that's bullshit, quite honestly, and I think that anyone who believes that is naive.

Don't get me wrong, I'm all for a Netflix binge day, but if you want shit to change in your life, business, whatever…

You need to do the work.

You need to sit your ass down and get shit done.

Plain and simple.

I love the hustle. I love the work. I love the grind.

I love to open up my laptop, start writing, start creating, start sharing. I could do it all day long if I didn't have other shit to do too!

So it's really no surprise that I spend the majority of my time "doing the work".

I eat, sleep, and breathe the hustle, and I'm not afraid to admit it!

I'm often called a workaholic because of how often I'm seen ignoring the world, nose deep in my work.

This used to bother me, because I didn't want people to think I was "addicted" to the computer/phone. I definitely didn't want them to think I was a bad mom/wife/sister/friend if I was seen on my phone in the company of others. Not anymore.

Although I try not to "work" when people are spending time with me, I won't be shamed into thinking that my doing so would somehow be wrong.

My true friends, my family...they get it. They get *me*. They support me.

Which means my hustle is not a problem for them (most of the time!).

Really, though, I do the work because I love the work. I do it because I can't *not*.

And through that hustle, I experience an ease that feels so good, I just wanna hustle some more.

The more I hustle, the easier the hustle feels.

When I, for some reason, can't get my hustle on, I feel antsy, out of sorts, and, in many cases, a bit pissed off.

I'm not "okay" again until I have had that time to really sit down and "do the work".

I love the hustle.

Truly. Madly. Deeply.

I believe in it.

I believe that it's important to work hard. I believe that a strong work ethic will take you far. I believe that if you put in the work, you will get the results.

I also believe that if you fall into the trap of believing that shit can't be easy, all of the time, that you are not gonna make it.

I believe you can have both. I believe you SHOULD have both.

My No-Holds-Barred Truth

Can I say something that may very well not make you happy?

Yes? Okay, thanks.

So, here's the truth, the real truth, and nothing but the truth:

Entrepreneurship is really fucking hard.

There will be many, *many* sleepless nights where you work your ass off. You may even get to a point where you forget what sleep actually IS, you miss so much of it.

I promise, you WILL sleep again.

Keep going.

There will be moments when you just want to curl up in a ball, cry your eyes out, and scream as loud as you possibly can, because all of your hard work went up in smoke.

Shit happens.

Keep going.

Your plans will fail.

Your business(es) will fail.

Your projects will fail.

Not all of them, of course, but many. Be prepared. Don't let the fear of failure keep you from taking action.

It's true: you will experience so many failures, you'll wonder why you even bother to keep going…and that's exactly what sets apart the successful from the unsuccessful.

The successful people in this world ended up being successful because they kept on getting up, every single time they were knocked down.

Failures, mistakes, problems…

They're all just lessons that will build you up to be bigger and stronger the next time.

All of the failures you experience in your entrepreneurial journey are for your good. Remember that. There is nothing that you can't handle.

You can weather the storm. You can get back up again. You can (and you will) succeed.

Failures show you what NOT to do next time.

Failures give you the opportunity to rise again and come back better than ever.

Failures allow you to get comfortable being uncomfortable (which is necessary for growth).

There isn't a single successful entrepreneur out there who hasn't failed at least once in their life, and more often there have been multiple failures.

So, yeah.

Being an entrepreneur is incredibly challenging. Aside from being a parent, it's the hardest gig I've ever had, but I wouldn't change it for anything.

It's made me who I am, which is a strong, resilient fighter, someone who knows what she's capable of.

Being an entrepreneur is also incredibly rewarding. Similar to watching your child grow up, watching your business grow and blossom into something big and impactful is so fulfilling.

That said, you need to do the work if you want to have the impact, if you want to make the money, and if you want to make the difference.

The work is a requirement. It's not something you can "get around".

You can't just "think happy thoughts" and visualize your desires coming true for you. You must also put in the blood, sweat, and tears.

The hustle, of course, is what I'm talking about.

You need it.

I've always believed in the hustle.

I've always believed that you must put in the work to get the results.

I've always believed that there will be hard days, and there will be days when you wonder how things got to be so easy, like you're not "working" at all.

Truth be told, my life now is easy. Really easy.

What My Day of "Hustle" Looks Like

It's 2 p.m., and since 5 a.m. this morning, I have:

Wrote in my journal.

Wrote two posts on Facebook.

Posted a few things to Instagram.

Made breakfast.

Took the kids to school.

Tracked my income and expenses.

Bought computer chairs for the office.

Ordered groceries for delivery.

Messaged back and forth with my clients.

Made lunch and watched *The Walking Dead.*

Did a livestream in the car, outside of the coffee shop.

Downloaded new music for my Spotify playlist.

Sang along to said music. (One of my favourite hobbies is finding a song with no vocals and then singing the lyrics really loud, pretending I'm a singer.)

Wrote this chapter for my book.

I didn't do these things because I had to. I did them because I wanted to. I listened to my gut, and I did what felt good in the moment.

This is how it always goes.

Every day, I just do what I want.

And in between lunches and singing and book writing, I'm also creating massive amounts of content for my online community, setting up new sales pages and Facebook ads for my offers, and engaging with my community on social media.

I'm doing "the work". The work which most people fail to do because they're too busy doing the stuff that doesn't actually matter (you know, like scrolling Facebook to see what "so and so" is up to, and taking course after course but not implementing what was taught).

If you were to spend the day with me, you'd probably comment that I "work too much", because I'm always GO, GO, GO, but the truth is, I just fell in love with the hustle.

I learned to love it in a way that it loves me back. Now, I am fueled by the hustle. The more I hustle, the more I WANT to hustle.

And so I do…

Again and again.

It's why I've been able to create the success I've had in my life and business. I did (and do) the freakin' work. Repeatedly.

It wasn't journaling that got me to where I am today.

It wasn't meditation either (in fact, I'm still not that great at meditation and often forget to do it).

It wasn't good luck, or knowing the "right people".

It was good old fashioned WORK.

Don't think that you can just waltz into entrepreneurship, align yourself with the people out there who tell you that it's supposed to be easy 100 percent of the time, and experience unlimited amounts of fortune and fame.

If it was supposed to be easy, everyone would be doing it.

But they aren't, because it's not.

It can *feel* easy, yes, but not until you learn to be a lover of the hustle.

Until then, it's gonna feel like a chore, and the more it feels like a chore, the more you will ignore it, and then your potential success goes out the window.

When it comes down to it, success is actually VERY simple.

Do the work. Love the work. Repeat. Daily.

Got it? Good. Now get outta here and go make shit happen!

Here's your homework:

1. Write the following "must-do's" down on a piece of paper and stick it to your computer. Do them every day.

- Content Creation (create it and share it)
- Sales Activity (actively ask for the sale)
- Money Work (track your income, expenses, debt, savings, investments, net worth, etc.)
- Community Growth & Engagement (do something that will grow your online community; also, engage with your current community)
- Mindset Work (whether journaling, visualization, meditation, or whatever else, daily inner work is crucial)

2. Decide on your top one to two goals for the next week. Write them down somewhere that you will see them each day. Do at least one task every day that will move you closer to achieving that goal(s).

3. Make a declaration to yourself that you will do whatever it takes, no matter what, until you achieve what you want to achieve. That you are committed to your success.

CHAPTER 10

GET HONEST WITH YOURSELF

You've read this book—yay!—so, now what?

What is your next step to get into the flow of life, to master your hustle, grow your biz, make an impact in the world, and crush your money goals, repeatedly?

We've talked about living life on your terms, making an income doing what you love, and now it's time for you to do some soul searching.

It's one thing to read a book and totally resonate with it, constantly nodding your head as you read along, but implementing the things that you learn here is what is really going to change things in your life and get you the things that you want.

CHANGE IS UP TO YOU

All of the a-ha moments you've had as you've read these words—have you written them down somewhere?

Have you made note of them in some way?

Or, better yet, have you implemented them?

Have you made them a part of your everyday actions?

Let me tell you, that is where the magic happens. It all comes to life when you take the things you learn and apply them to your life.

Otherwise, you're just reading for fun, which is totally cool of course, but I want you to get results—some kind of big win—from this.

I want you to take what you read, apply what resonates with you to your life, and reap the rewards.

I want you to thrive, to make a difference, to grow this business and life of yours into an empire that you're wildly obsessed with.

What do you want?

Do you want to continue staying where you are, dreaming about what you really want, but never actually having or experiencing it?

Or do you want to slay your business, your money, your life—all of it?

Can you truly say that, right now, you're living your ideal life?

If your answer is no, you have some work to do.

It's time to blow shit up and re-build, this time in a way that actually makes a difference, that gets you to your goal.

You feel me?

One thing I've noticed with a lot of the "entrepreneurs" who pop up online every day is that most of them are lacking one very important skill:

Resilience.

They're lacking the resilience to get up, day after day, and do the work. They're looking for the easy button that they can hit and see their badass dream business come to life in front of them.

They try, sure they try, but they fail—as we all do from time to time, it's part of the territory—and what do they all do?

They quit.

"Fuck this, it doesn't work."

"I can't be bothered anymore."

"This is way too hard."

"I invested all of my money and it didn't work, so now I'm broke. I give up."

And they bow out.

Back to the online job boards to try and find a paycheck that they deem is "stable" and "reliable", but is anything but.

What they're missing is the guts to get back up again.

To keep on swinging, even when they feel like they've got nothing left.

What they're missing is the passion that jolts them awake in bed each morning, fueled with desire to get up and make shit happen.

What they're missing is the relentless fire that burns within them 24 hours a day, 7 days a week, 365 days a year.

What they don't realize is that this is what it takes.

It takes getting burned.

It takes missing sleep.

It takes pushing hard every day.

It takes doing the hard things.

It takes getting punched in the face repeatedly.

It takes losing and winning and winning and losing.

It takes getting hit over and over, and consistently getting back up and screaming LOUDER.

This is what it takes, and if you don't have the guts to go through it, to embrace it, to have a passion and resilience so strong that every time shit gets hard you yell, "is that all you've got?!" And you keep on going.

You wouldn't be reading this book if you didn't have this inside of you.

I know you've got it. You know you've got it.

The only question now is, are you willing to use it?

Are you willing to use your voice to say the things you know you're meant to say, even when it seems like everyone else disagrees with you?

Will you stand up for your yourself, for your beliefs?

Are you willing to stay the course, no matter how bumpy, how painful, how fucking HARD it gets?

Will you do the work, will you try, try again, every time you get knocked down?

Are you willing to believe in yourself so much that, even though it seems like everyone around you is encouraging you to quit because "it won't work" and "it's too risky", you keep going anyway?

Are you willing to take the risk on yourself, again and again?

The only way you will experience the success that you want in life, no matter what it is, how big or small is if you repeatedly do the things you know you must.

So, let me ask you:

Are you willing to do what it takes? Are you willing to show up—all the way up—for your dreams?

Are you willing to do it even when you're scared, do it when you're uncertain, do it no matter how messy it gets?

Until you are, you'll always feel like a hamster going 'round and 'round on that wheel, until you get so dizzy that you puke and give up.

Because you will.

Ain't no one crazy enough to keep on spinning, over and over, forever.

So you can choose to be successful, to live the life of your dreams, doing all that you know how in order to get there.

Or, of course, you can stay stuck in that quicksand that is sucking you in, deeper and deeper every day, as you ignore what your soul is telling you to do. Which is to get the fuck up and move, bitch.

Do the damn thing.

All the damn things.

Push. Pull. Push. Pull.

It's the requirement of success, and one that so few are willing to do. Don't be those few.

Be the one who rises up, every morning, every afternoon, every night, and makes things happen.

I've noticed that the more someone wants something, the more likely they are to show up and take action on it every day.

They will do it no matter how afraid they are.

No matter how uncertain they are of their next move.

They just keep showing up, one foot in front of the other, daily, no exceptions.

Can you honestly say that you really, truly, want the thing you keep saying you want? Or is it someone else's idea of success that you're holding onto? Someone else's dream you're chasing?

What to Do if You're Not Living Your Ideal Life

Can you truly say, with absolute certainty, that you're doing what you know you were born to do?

If not, it's time to shape up, take a look inside of your soul, and ask the hard questions:

What do I really want?

What does my ideal life look like? My ideal business?

Whom do I want to be surrounded by?

How much money do I want to be making? Why do I want this money?

How do I want to be spending my time?

How will I know that I'm fulfilling my life's purpose?

How will I know that I've achieved success? What does "success" actually look like to me?

In what ways am I sabotaging my success right now?

What or who can I eliminate from my life in order to achieve the things that I want and live the life that I desire?

What kind of friends do I want in my life?

What kind of relationships do I want to have?

What do my ideal mornings look like? Evenings? Weekends?

What am I doing every day that I don't want to be doing?

What can I outsource in my life and business, so that I can focus on doing what I'm meant do to?

And, most importantly, how am I holding myself back, and what do I need to do to knock that shit off?

Have you ever truly taken the time (and sometimes it takes a lot of time) to observe your life and identify how you're fucking shit up?

How you're saying NO to your desires?

How you're slowing down your potential for success?

Have you ever really, truly let go of all your inhibitions and gone after what you want?

If not, why?

Do you not trust yourself?

Do you not believe in yourself?

Or maybe you're confused as all hell and don't even know how to begin?

All of this stuff is important to know, to understand, and then, of course, to shift.

This is why I am such a strong advocate of journaling. It allows you to dig within your soul and take a good look at what's going on inside of you.

It allows you to see what you're doing, what you're thinking, what you're believing, what you're asking for, and, ultimately, what you're receiving and experiencing.

The One Daily Activity that Can Change Your Life

If you're not journaling on the daily, I encourage you to start—even if all you write is a few sentences each day.

Just start. It will evolve over time.

Ask yourself the questions—the hard ones and the easy ones—every day.

Don't let a day go by without picking up your pen and letting your thoughts flow from inside your head onto the paper.

Explore what's going on inside your mind, and use that knowledge for good.

Use it to change the way you're doing things, if the way you're doing things isn't helping you to get what you want.

Use it to identify what it is you actually desire in life and affirm it as done, because it is. You just need to line up WITH it, so you can then receive it.

How many Januarys are you going to make the same resolutions, only to bail halfway through the month?

How many dreams are you going to abandon before you even begin?

How many times are you going to say "no" to your soul, when your soul is begging you to say "yes"?

The sad truth is that most people sabotage themselves when they're terrified of the success they're so close to experiencing.

TOP 3 WAYS YOU SABOTAGE YOUR SUCCESS

1. You let other people talk you out of your dreams.

They tell you that your dreams are too big, too hard, or impossible, and you believe them.

Instead: Thank them for their opinion, and then ignore it. Keep doing what you know you're here to do. The only opinion that matters is yours. Not your mom's, not your partner's. Just yours.

2. You let your fear of success stop you from going after the "really big things" you desire.

For whatever reason, you're scared of getting "there", where success is yours (use the questions I asked you above to determine what you're afraid of).

Instead: Trust that the desires you have are meant for you, otherwise you wouldn't have them. Every day, write out how grateful you are for your massive success. Embrace it. Love it. Appreciate it. And keep chasing it.

3. You refuse to do the work, because you don't know how, or what, or where, or when, or blah blah blah (insert excuse of your choice here).

You do the bare minimum. You ignore the impulses you have to do something else, something more, something next level—which keeps you stuck, exactly where you are right now, forever.

Instead: Always do more than the bare minimum, even if it's just one extra task that you tackle each day. If you don't know what to do or how to do it, give yourself the gift of help from a mentor. Do the work, do the work, do the work.

Here's the truth:

There is only one way to succeed, to receive all the things you want in life, and to live in a way that feels good, that excites you, that inspires you (and others):

You need to keep on showing up.

You need to keep on taking action.

You need to keep on keeping on, day after day, over and over, until you have everything that you've ever wanted—at which point, you dream even bigger, and you keep on going!

That's the thing with people like you, with people like US...

We're never truly satisfied. Grateful for it all, but always wanting more.

The chase is what we love. The hustle is what we crave. The doing is what we're REALLY after.

Yeah, the results are nice. The big, shiny things we achieve and receive in our life are wonderful, but they're not actually what we're into.

We're into the journey.

We're into the making of things.

We're into the act of *doing*.

And that's what the OTHERS will never understand, and that's why they will never, ever, be one of us—because they don't know how.

They can't even grasp the concept of this.

Of the joy that comes from doing the work.

Of the passion that fills you up every day, to the point where you feel like you're going to explode if someone gets too close to you.

The others, the normals, the regular people who actually enjoy a life of mediocrity...

That's just not who we are. Nor who we ever *want* to be.

This is why it's absolutely critical to do life your own way, to run this business your own way, because doing it any other way would be success suicide.

You can't allow the negativity from others to infect you.

You can't allow the naysayers to sway you from doing what you know you're meant to do.

You can't allow critics to tear you down and keep you small.

You have to rise above all of that (and other) bullshit and do your thing, no matter what obstacles stand in your way (and there will be many of them!).

You are in control of your life. You get to choose how it all turns out. You get to choose what happens, and what doesn't.

It's all up to you. So what are you doing letting others get in the way?

What are you doing agreeing with people who tell you that your dreams are too big, too risky, too irresponsible?

What are you doing giving up on the dreams you know are meant for you?

What are you *doing*?

More importantly: what are you going to do *now*?

The choice is always yours, and you can make a new choice right now, to one that actually serves you.

You no longer have to stay at this same level, where you feel so small, where it doesn't feel right at all.

You can choose to elevate. To begin again. To dream bigger.

You can choose, at any time, to be relentless in pursuit of your desires.

You have all that you need inside of you. The passion, the power, the motivation, the answers…you have everything.

It's time you tap into it.

It's time you do this thing.

Believe in yourself. Trust yourself. And, finally:

Leap.

CONCLUSION

I hope by this point, you've really grasped the concept that you can do business, life, everything on your terms.

You don't have to do things any other way than the way that feels best to you.

You really can be, do and have everything you want, so long as you commit to it and take action every day to make it real.

It's so important for me to get across to you the point that you have all of the potential inside of you. There is so much good inside of you that you're meant to release into the world.

You have important work to do.

You have so many lives to touch.

You have so many amazing things to experience in your life, and I hope that you give yourself permission to do them.

You are worthy of living a life you absolutely adore, where you get to spend your days doing only what you love, being fully supported in all areas, making an impact, and having total freedom and abundance in all areas.

You can have it all. You really can.

Don't stop until it's yours—and then keep going! The universe has such incredible things in store for you, and the more you show up, the more you are present, the more you will receive.

So live your life, live it boldly, live it fully, and know—deep down—that everything you desire is meant for you.

If you crave support in building your business into one you are madly in love with, I would love to help you!

You can check the resources page at the back of this book for a list of free trainings that I've created for you. If you're ready to go to the next level and want to work together privately, find me on www. cassiehoward.com or social media, and let's chat!

My passion is to support rebellious entrepreneurs who have a badass streak and who want to make incredible money doing what they love, while living a life of purpose and influence.

If we're a good fit, you already know.

If we're meant to work together, you already know.

If we're supposed to be besties who hustle from our laptops around the world, while eating copious amounts of vegan food in our pajamas, you already know.

Reach out to me. Let's chat. I'd absolutely love to talk with you!

You have so much goodness inside of you, and you're doing the world a disservice when you keep it all to yourself.

The world needs your magic.

The worst possible thing you can do is refuse to release it. For you. For the world.

You are so fucking important. I don't care what you were told in the past. I don't care what people are telling you now. I don't care what the voices in your head are trying to convince you of.

The truth is this:

There are so many people in the world who need you. So many who are just waiting for you to make an entrance into their life. So many who so badly desire your knowledge, your support, your guidance, your love.

You are wanted. You are loved.

All you need to do now?

Show the world who you are, and change lives just by being you.

Your needs will be met. Your desires will be fulfilled. The path to which you will manifest these needs and desires will be revealed to you as soon as you step into your power and be the you that you were always meant to be.

The moment you accept and love yourself for who you really are is the moment your life will change.

The world needs your voice.

The world needs your magic.

The world needs YOU.

It's time for you to show up and claim the spotlight.

Cheering for you,

Cassie

FIND ME ONLINE:

Facebook: @cassiehowardbiz
Instagram: @cassiehowardbiz
Website: www.cassiehoward.com

Printed in Great Britain
by Amazon